# GIMME SHELTER

*A Tail of Anger, Rescue, and Redemption*

## Louis Spirito

*Gimme Shelter.* Copyright © 2013 by Louis Spirito

*All Rights Reserved. No part of this book may be used or reproduced in any electronic or mechanical means, including information storage and retrieval systems, without written permission, except in the case of brief quotations embodied in critical articles or reviews.*

Library of Congress 20139002244

Spirito, Louis

*Gimme Shelter*

ISBN 978-0-9890578-2-0

For Eugenie and Tanner.

My goal is to become the man you both deserve

*Eugenie, Lou, and Tanner*

*"You can't always get what you want...*
*But if you try sometimes you just might find...*
*You get what you need."*
　　　*—The Rolling Stones*

*Tanner, an American Dog*

# CONTENTS

| | |
|---|---|
| PREFACE | 9 |
| CHAPTER 1: BIG RED DOGS—"Rebel" | 12 |
|     ADOPTING A RESCUE DOG: Things to Consider | 23 |
| CHAPTER 2: BIG RED DOGS—"Reggie" | 26 |
|     PET INSURANCE: Luxury Or Necessity? | 31 |
| CHAPTER 3: BACK ON THE HORSE | 34 |
|     "DOMINANT" BREEDS & PIT BULLS | 44 |
| CHAPTER 4: A VERY ANGRY GUY | 45 |
|     PREVENTING DOG AGGRESSION | 65 |
| CHAPTER 5: "FIRST" THINGS FIRST | 70 |
| CHAPTER 6: JUNE GLOOM | 91 |
|     DOGS & RATTLESNAKES | 109 |
| CHAPTER 7: GOING HOME | 111 |
| CHAPTER 8: TOO SCARY TO LIVE WITH | 123 |
|     THE ODDS OF BEING KILLED BY A PIT BULL | 144 |
| CHAPTER 9: SCHOOL DAZE | 146 |
|     FINDING A DOG TRAINER | 173 |
| CHAPTER 10: REDEMPTION | 176 |
|     NUMBER OF DOGS & PIT BULLS EUTHANIZED ANNUALLY | 187 |
| CHAPTER 11: THE HOLIDAYS | 188 |
| CHAPTER 12: WATER, WATER EVERYWHERE | 200 |

| | |
|---|---|
| DOGS & HEATSTROKE | 217 |
| CHAPTER 13: FULL CIRCLE | 221 |
| ACKNOWLEDGEMENTS | 228 |
| APPENDIX #1: DOG RESCUE RESOURCES | 230 |
| APPENDIX #2: ANGER MANAGEMENT RESOURCES | 232 |
| ABOUT THE AUTHOR | 234 |

# PREFACE

Until we rescued Tanner, I'd never kept a journal of any kind. Suddenly, for reasons I still don't fully understand, I found myself recording the minutiae (nearly 500 pages worth!) of my daily interactions with a timid, homeless Pit Bull we'd plucked from the shelter.

We had heard the horror stories about seemingly docile house pets mauling and even murdering their owners and other innocent victims for no apparent reason. But Tanner was a far cry from the schizoid, hair-trigger killers portrayed by the fear-mongering media. He was gentle, loving, intelligent, and eager to please: quite simply the best, sweetest dog I'd ever known. Although we were just getting started, knowing how quickly time slips by, I wanted and needed a tangible reminder of our journey together before it was done.

As the pages began to pile up, I started to drift back to what seemed like another lifetime, to the raucous days (and nights) of my 20s and 30s, when I lived in New York City with another terrific dog. I was in a different, and better, place now, yet a part of me longed to recapture the madcap energy and exhilaration of my youthful misadventures. I secretly hoped that Tanner would help me do that. I soon realized, however, that he was leading me instead on a different but critical voyage of self-discovery. That's when a second, strange impulse took hold: to turn my diary into a book.

I'd published some short non-fiction and had a few minor successes writing screenplays, but a story about my messy relationship with this dog? To do it honestly, I would have to expose a side of myself that I'd worked hard to hide: my addiction to anger. I'd also have to explain how I came to be so angry. That would mean discussing my family and our contentious dynamics. Printing house catalogs are chock full of whiny memoirs pointing fingers and assigning blame for lives gone awry. I didn't feel like adding to the pile, especially when some of the parties were no longer alive to defend themselves.

There was also a dramatic concern. While my anger had taken a terrible emotional toll on me and on people whom I hold dear, it hadn't wrought the kind of spectacular flameout that garners headlines. I hadn't been shot for disrespecting a mob boss, or been bounced from my job as a studio head only to wind up washing windshields on the Bowery. Mine was just the story of a relatively normal man who'd succumbed to a powerful, all-too-common destructive impulse. Who would care? Who would listen? The whole idea of a book seemed daunting and I was already battling to keep my demons in check.

But the more that I dismissed the notion, the stronger it grew. By recounting my journey, I'd be shining a light on a serious issue that plagued not just me but countless other men, women and children. Because my life was "ordinary," it would be difficult for readers to dismiss the lessons that I'd been forced to learn.

Dealing with rage is a complicated matter that often requires professional help. Tanner's story wouldn't be "the answer," but hearing about the struggles of his immature owner might serve as a starting point, a gentle nudge toward recognition of the problem.

At the same time, I'd be pleading the case for a host of unjustly maligned Pit Bulls and other "vicious" dogs sitting on death row in shelters across the country. If my effort saved just one, it would be worth it. In the end, sharing the story of our journey wasn't so much a choice as a compulsion; it seemed the right thing, the only thing, to do.

Louis Spirito<br>
Malibu, California

# CHAPTER 1
# BIG RED DOGS—"Rebel"

*I'm four, maybe five-years-old. We've just returned from a party with the Spirito clan, an all-day extravaganza with enough baked clams, lasagna, and steak to feed an army division. My parents are into it again, cursing, and shouting, and screaming full bore. It's like this a lot, but today it's extra nasty. My mother's on the rampage, charged up because my father's getting dressed, heading out to drop another small fortune at some back room craps game. Or maybe just to see "The Polack," his steady girlfriend. He threatens, but she keeps spitting insults until, finally, all hell breaks loose. My sister, brother, and I rush between them, crying, "We hate you! We hate you! We hate you!" until he turns and stalks out. Oh, by the way, it's Christmas.*

~~

**Blanche**

It was late November 2008, and Blanche, our Scottish Fold, had reached the end of the line. Before she joined our menagerie, I'd never owned a cat. Never wanted to. From the time I was a boy, I was strictly a dog person. Then, one day, there she was, this tiny puff of gray fur, a surprise "gift" from my mother-in-law who found her to be odd-looking.

She was. Blanche had a huge, moon-shaped head and the flopped-over ears typical of her breed. She was also fearless. Despite her diminutive stature, she hijacked a choice spot on the sofa alongside of our dogs, Rebel and Roxanne, who regarded her as though she was a mountain lion. When she grew tired of intimidating them, she moved on to George, the cockatiel, and spent hours perched beside his cage, letting the frantic bird comb her whiskers with his beak.

Blanche had the howl of a tiger and the personality of a hermit monk. As a youngster, she tolerated cuddling but only if we first cradled her inside of a cardboard box or paper bag. It took ten years of coaxing before she grudgingly let us fondle her without protection. By then, the dogs were gone, George had flown back to his original home, and we'd fallen in love with our kooky little cat. Now, at sixteen, her kidneys had quit. Deaf and nearly blind, she couldn't cross the room without stumbling.

Blanche was nestled in my lap, purring gently, as we drove to the vet's in stiff-lipped silence. When we got there, I swaddled her in my sweatshirt and carried her inside. The vet confirmed our decision: it was time to say goodbye. We fed her Pounce, cooed her name, and it was done. A chapter was finished.

With Blanche's passing, my wife and I quickly realized that a house with no animals was just too quiet for us. As we toasted our cantankerous girl with a glass of Chianti, we fell to reminiscing about former pets. We realized that it had been thirteen years since we'd last had a dog of our own. We love dogs and take every chance we get to invite them into our world. So why had we waited so long? And where had the time gone?

After Christmas and New Year's slipped past, I began to send out feelers to various online rescue groups that sought homes for their millions of cuddly, loveable dogs in all shapes and sizes. We'd discussed our preferences. Big and athletic were good. No pocket pooches, no hyper breeds, and definitely no Dalmatians (more on that later). We agreed to stay open minded but, deep down inside, I didn't want just any mutt. I wanted an Irish Setter like the one I'd had when we first met, a jaunty, rollicking dog that would help me recapture the excitement of my days as a struggling actor who was living the *vida loca* of sex, drugs & disco in the wonderland that was NYC.

For some men, a mid-life crisis means a mistress or a Maserati. All I wanted was a big red dog, a four-legged time machine to take me back to an era before mortgages, life insurance, and prostate exams, a time of overlooked possibilities and squandered opportunities. I wanted a do-over.

~~~

It was a rainy weekend in late February 2009. I'd gone to the market and returned to find Eugenie waiting for me in the garage. She was clutching the phone and beaming like we'd won the lottery. The news was even better. We'd just received a call from a rescue group about a year-old Setter that needed a home. Reggie had lived with a family—dad, mom, and young twin boys—for almost a year. They'd tolerated his puppy antics, but ultimately he'd worn out his welcome when he tripped and injured the mother. They needed to place him ASAP. Were we interested? I bolted upstairs, phoned back, and filed an application. That evening, we went dancing to celebrate. Early the next morning, we were on our way to Upland, CA to bring him home.

~~~

Reggie would be our second "rescue Setter." In 1983, while I was living in Greenwich Village, I'd adopted his predecessor: an amazing dog named Rebel. I hadn't planned on having a dog. I hadn't planned on living in New York, either.

Several years earlier, I was teaching English in New Jersey when a friend, who worked the line at General Motors, asked whether I would join him for an acting class in Manhattan. I'd never considered performing before. Caught in the throes of a busted romance, I figured "what the hell"; at the very least I'd meet some hot new women. After a few weeks, though, the novelty wore off and my friend quit. I stayed and caught the acting bug.

When I wasn't grading papers or scoring tests, I drove into The City for singing, speech, and dance classes. I used up sick days to audition for regional theatre and off-off-Broadway shows. It was just a lark at first. Then I started to land small roles, working for free in obscure storefronts and lofts. On show nights, we'd finish north of 10:00 PM. I'd take my bow, race back across the Hudson River, hurriedly plan the next day's lessons, and then crash in a heap until the alarm exploded at 6:00 the next morning.

Juggling my job and my passion was exciting, and exhausting. I took naps in the break room at school. I swigged coffee by the gallon waiting for my cues backstage. Something had to give. An actor friend offered a solution: a job working the door at a disco that he managed on Lower Fifth Avenue, across from the Lone Star Cafe. If I took the gig, I'd be free to concentrate on acting. I hesitated; there was no tenure at the club. Richie sensed my trepidation. He'd been a teacher, too, and once faced a similar quandary. So he proposed a trial run; I could try out the nightlife, and keep my teaching job.

The new school year had just begun, and there I was, cramming Shakespeare down the gullets of bored, suburban high schoolers from 8:00-3:00, treading the boards in Renaissance garb from 7:00-10:30, then manning the velvet rope from 11:00-3:00 AM, and sleeping three hours a night. Two weeks of this marathon madness brought me to my knees. I met with the English Coordinator and offered my resignation.

The new gig didn't pay well, but the "benefits" made up for it. This was pre-AIDS New York, the time of Studio 54, Andy Warhol, cocaine, Quaaludes, and casual sex. I spent my nights with "fabulous" people, had an endless supply of free drugs, and fooled around with scores of exotic, sophisticated women. Working at the club was an aphrodisiac. I didn't understand it—I was the same as before—but I took advantage of my newfound allure. Theatre? Forget it. I was too tired, and my voice was too shredded from partying to even audition. I didn't care. Why bother working to be a star when I already lived like one? This enervating fling lasted three tumultuous years until a family tragedy brought me back to my senses. And back to acting.

I escaped from the dark side, but I still had to feed myself. I got a hack license and started driving a cab at Dover Garage on Hudson Street, the colorful location that TV viewers might recognize from the hit sitcom *Taxi*. Like the show, the actual garage featured a surly dispatcher who shook down his drivers at every turn. If you wanted to work that shift, you paid for the privilege. If you wanted a new car that would make it through the night, you slipped him a five when you handed in your license. Air conditioning on a summer day? Another $5. During busy weeks, like those around the Christmas holidays, "Ozzie" probably netted a cool two grand in payoffs, cash.

Not surprisingly, Ozzie hardly ever called in sick. On those rare occasions that he went AWOL, John, one of the office staff, pinch hit. As I handed in my card on a crisp September afternoon, John asked if I knew anyone who might want an Irish Setter. He was holding the dog for a friend who had to give him up, and the hapless beast was marking time in a vet's office in Queens. I told him that I'd ask around.

I called my sister, an investigator with the Hudson County, New Jersey Prosecutor's Office, and relayed the story. She said that one of her colleagues was looking for a dog for his kids. He'd be happy to take the Setter as soon as he finished moving. I gave John the message and forgot about it.

A week later, he broached the subject again. Boarding costs were mounting rapidly, and he really needed to place the dog right away. It was either that or leave him at a city shelter where he would remain until adopted or put down. I reluctantly agreed to keep him in my studio apartment until his new home became available. I called my sister who promised to touch base with her fellow detective and get back to me.

Growing up in Elizabeth, NJ, some twenty miles and a light year from Manhattan, we'd always had dogs. The first was Victory, a stray mutt that wandered into the family restaurant on V-E Day.

He pilfered a string of sausage and hunkered down under a booth, daring anyone to reclaim his prize. My grandfather took a shine to him, and he quickly became a fixture at the tavern, diligently inspecting every man in uniform who stopped by, searching for a master who never came home from the War.

Ostensibly, Victory lived with my family. In reality, he came and went as pleased. When he wanted a change in menu, he'd call on the neighbors who treated him like a friend. And when he grew tired of roaming the streets, "whoring around" as my mom put it, he'd visit the dog warden, a loyal customer who'd drive him home as she made her rounds. Vickie stuck around until my brother arrived (the third of four kids), then he wandered off to meet his end like some old Sioux chief.

After Victory came Sally, a sweet, lovable shmoo of a mutt, that slept in the washing machine. And Petey, a black-eyed hound that ran like the wind and went to live with my younger sister when the rest of us lit out for wider, if not greener, pastures. Toss in a couple of ill-fated puppies, (one caught distemper and had to be destroyed; another fell victim to a car), and I felt more than qualified for some short-term dog sitting.

I followed John to the top floor of the garage where Village residents, too lazy to cope with alternate side of the street parking or too tired of paying the steep tow-away fines, forked over a small fortune to stow their battered cars. He disappeared into the office and reappeared with a small, red horse. His tail wagging as it would until his last breath, the mini-Secretariat dragged John across the oil-spattered concrete floor, stopping only to deposit a huge, steaming mound. John scooped up the mess and tossed it away. The next one would be on me. I vowed right then that Rebel's stay with me would be brief.

It had to be. When I wasn't taking classes, going on auditions, or mounting productions at the off-off Broadway company that I'd founded with some fellow actors, I was out "whoring around with the legion of club girls that I'd met prior to my cab driving penance. When things went well, I stayed out all night; if they went really well, sometimes all week. Having a dog that needed walking might offer a convenient escape from a date gone bad. It could also torpedo any spontaneous trysts.

I wasn't scheduled to work that evening and had forgotten to check my calendar. When I did, I discovered that I'd made plans with a fiery Nuyorican model to see rockabilly artist Robert Gordon at a local club. Afterward, I figured that we'd grab a drink. Then we'd hunker down at her place for some *amor caliente*.

I took Rebel for a walk around 10:00 PM. Or, rather, he took me, hauling me all over the neighborhood like a whaleboat on a Nantucket sleigh ride. Disheveled and exhausted, I set off to meet my Latina hottie. As I left the apartment, the last thing I saw was his long, narrow face staring up at me.

At noon the following day, I stuck my key in the lock. I braced for disaster. At very least, the dog had watered my hardwood floors. At worst... The door swung open and there he was, seated where I'd left him, his big, soulful brown eyes filled with relief, and panic. I grabbed the leash, rushed him outside, and stood back as he flooded the gutter.

His Zen-like restraint impressed me. In the span of twenty-four hours he'd been hauled out of a kennel where he'd spent the past month, moved to a garage, dumped in a strange apartment, been left alone overnight, and still managed to control himself. A dangerous thought crept into my sleep-deprived brain: this dog's a keeper. I called my sister and told her the deal was off; Rebel was staying with me.

He had had four owners in his first three years. That night, as he stretched out on his side of the bed, I assured him that I would be his last. He seemed pleased with that and nodded off, leaving me to ponder all the yet-unconquered beauties that I'd never meet. Getting Rebel proved to be a turning point of sorts. By taking a chance on the dog, I'd shifted my old patterns and opened up to new possibilities. Two weeks later, I had my first date with Eugenie, another red-haired keeper who would eventually become my wife.

As promised, Reb lived out his days with us, surviving our yearly prenuptial breakups, a foul-tempered Dalmatian named Roxanne, and our move from NYC to Malibu. He died in his sleep at the age of fourteen but not before one final act of loyalty.

To mark our fifth anniversary, we had planned a trip to Italy where we were married. A week before our departure, Reb suffered a stroke that left him wobbly and too weak to eat. We considered putting him down or canceling our trip. It didn't seem right to dump our burden on the kindly neighbor who had offered to dog-sit. In a last ditch effort, the vet prescribed prednisone. Rebel rallied. We went off to Ravello for limoncello and gelato.

The Amalfi Coast drips romance, but Reb's condition cast a dark cloud on our holiday. There were no cell phones then, and we came home expecting the worst. When we opened the door, he rushed to greet us, his tail swishing merrily just like always. We were overjoyed.

The next morning, he couldn't lift his head. His breathing was shallow and ragged, the spirit gone out of him like a pinpricked blow-up toy. We'd run out of miracles. I called the vet and made the appointment. Then I hung up the phone and went to get my coat. By the time I made it back upstairs, he was gone.

The timing of Rebel's passing was probably just coincidence. Then again, perhaps not. Perhaps he'd hung on, true to the end, waiting to see our faces one last time, just to make sure that we were okay. Mission accomplished, he'd gracefully surrendered, sparing us that awful decision. It didn't matter; we were still crushed. His ashes sat on a shelf in the vet's office for nearly a year before we had recovered enough to retrieve them.

***Rebel***

## *ADOPTING A RESCUE DOG: Things to Consider*

**First Time Dog Owners Should:**
- ▶ Find a local veterinarian and discuss canine nutrition and healthcare needs such a checkups and vaccinations. Medical emergencies can be expensive, so you might want to inquire about pet insurance.
- ▶ Visit a pet store and familiarize yourself with the basics (leashes, collars, beds, training crates, food, treats, shampoo) to get a sense of what your expenses will be.
- ▶ If you work long hours or travel frequently, check with local boarding kennels and dog walkers to ask about their rates.

**All Dog Owners Should:**
- ▶ Consider your needs and abilities. Ask yourself what you want/need in a dog. Will the dog be your constant companion? Will it have to co-exist with young children? With other dogs or cats? Does your apartment, condo or co-op board have any size or breed restrictions?
- ▶ Spend some time researching the breed you are considering. Learn what it was bred for and the breed's general temperament. If you live in a small apartment and aren't big on outdoor exercise, you might want to avoid a dog that was bred for running. If you are away at work during the day and the dog will be indoors, you might want to consider a low-energy dog. A good

resource is *The ASPCA Complete Guide to Dogs*. The more knowledge you have, the better your chances for a successful pairing.

▶ Decide how much time and energy you are willing to devote to the dog. Many people overestimate both. As a result, the dog gets shortchanged on exercise and affection, or becomes a burden to the owners, making a failed adoption more likely. Puppies and young dogs generally require more time and patience than older ones.

**People With Children Should:**

▶ Include all family members in the selection of the dog. Bringing home a new dog can be chaotic in the best of circumstances. Defining each member's responsibilities *before* adoption will help lessen the chaos. Young children may be too physically aggressive for very young puppies or fragile toy breeds. A dog that growls, cowers, raises its hackles, runs from your children, or that is reluctant to be petted is probably not a good choice for families with children.

**At The Shelter:**

▶ Spend at least one hour getting to know the dog you are considering. Barring unforeseen events, this animal will be a member of your family for 12 or more years.

- ▶ Ideally, make multiple visits to the shelter at various times of the day to observe the dogs you are considering. A dog that seems cute and laid back on one occasion might be aggressive and keyed up on another. Shelter conditions are less than ideal. A shy or overactive dog may just be responding to the stress of shelter life.
- ▶ Ask the staff about the dog you are considering. Was it surrendered or a stray? If the former, ask to see the intake sheet that may contain the dog's medical history and other useful information. Observe the dog around other dogs to see how it behaves. If you are seeking an affectionate dog, it should be affectionate at the shelter.

**Resources**

- Tony Rollins, Tony Rollins K-9 Academy
- Rob Lerner, CPDT-KA
- ASPCA, "Adopting A Shelter Dog"
- PetFinder.com, "Things To Consider Before You Adopt a Dog"
- Partnership For Animal Welfare, "Before You Decide To Adopt A Dog"
- Dr. Howie Baker, DVM

# CHAPTER 2
# BIG RED DOGS—"Reggie"

*Life wasn't always ugly and I wasn't always angry. I know because I have the photos from before my sisters and brother were born, when it was just my parents, our dog, Vickie, and me. In one picture, I'm a baby, cradled in my parents' arms. They're beaming, a happy family with no sign of the rancor that would soon follow and envelope us all. It would be years before I'd glimpse that peace again, tortured years full of sadness, rage, and shame.*

**The writer with his parents, 1951**

Like Rebel, Reggie was big and sweet. Unlike Reb, he was very hyper; think the Energizer Bunny on Red Bull. We went to fetch him in a Chrysler convertible, the larger of our two cars. His kennel was so huge—I have friends in New York whose apartments are smaller—that we had to take it apart and lower the top in order to wedge it into the rear seat. Even then, the disassembled crate took up so much space that Reggie had to ride crouched down inside of it. He wasn't thrilled. It was raining heavily and the freeway was a mess. We spent the two-hour drive fighting to keep the manic dog from diving into the front seat and forcing us off the road.

Back home, we quickly discovered that Reggie was a quintessential wild thing. He played nonstop, chewed anything in his path, and demolished the house if left unsupervised. Following The Dog Whisperer's credo of exercise, discipline and affection, I walked him for forty minutes every morning before breakfast. A brisk stroll of that length would tire most dogs. For Reggie it was merely the prelude to an hour of balls-out fetch with his stuffed duck. Strong and spirited, he loved to roughhouse, and would gnaw Eugenie's arm like a pull-toy. Yelling, "Stop!" only revved him up further.

In short order, we baby-proofed the house. We started showering in shifts, taking care that one of us was with him at all times. When that wasn't possible, I secured him to the metal railing with a steel cable. We felt like prison guards, always on alert, always shouting orders. After two weeks, we'd lost several pounds and were too exhausted to fool around, which was a first for us. These minor obstacles aside, we'd started to bond with the big lug.

We were prepared to gut it out until he calmed down or we died trying. Then, things took an unexpected and unfortunate turn.

From the moment that we first saw him, we noticed that Reggie's lower eyelids were very loose and red, like the English actor Michael Gambon, if he were a dog. "Molly," our rescue contact, assured us that the eye thing was normal with Setters; that being a young male he would eventually "grow into his head." Rebel never looked like that, but we deferred to her expertise and put it out of our minds.

By the end of week two, Reggie's eyes were badly swollen, puffed up like a fighter who'd forgotten how to duck. They were so sensitive that he yelped if we accidentally touched them. It hurt just to look at him. We took him to our vet, Dr. Lisa, a kind woman who'd helped our kitty Blanche make a graceful exit. She dismissed the business about the drooping lids being normal, and she consulted a colleague, a canine ophthalmologist. They concurred that Reggie had a serious, chronic eye ailment, one that would require ongoing, costly care for the rest of his life. We were stunned, and torn.

Neither of us wanted the pressure of doctoring a sick animal, especially a large, unruly one. If you know going in that you're getting a special needs dog, or if a family pet develops a serious but treatable illness, then you step up and do what you have to do. With Reggie, however, we'd been assured that we were getting a healthy, adoptable dog, which clearly wasn't the case. On top of that, our financial ship was already leaky. A hefty monthly vet bill might very well sink us.

For two tortured days we seesawed back and forth. Then we called Molly and told her that we were sending Reggie back. She was annoyed; she'd have to find him another home, and do it on short notice. We were upset, too, particularly when we learned that she had never personally inspected the dog. If she had, she might have noticed his problem and been in a position to disclose it to us beforehand, giving us the opportunity to say, "no thanks." Now that we'd begun to bond with him, we felt guilty and sad. We offered to re-adopt him if the problem could be cured but, deep down, we both knew that our time with this big red dog was over.

The return trip to Upland felt like a funeral procession. When we reached the vet's, we solemnly unloaded Reggie's crate, bed, and food. I took him inside and surrendered him to the receptionist. She led him away, tail wagging happily. He never looked back.

For a few days we kept in touch with Molly, who informed us that another rescue organization had stepped in to pay for Reggie's treatment, which had already totaled several thousand dollars. During our final conversation we were relieved to hear that she had placed Reggie with a lady vet who worked at the facility where he was being treated. The woman had just lost her thirteen-year-old Setter and was thrilled to have the new boy. So, sad as we were, and we were very sad, we knew that it was all for the best. She would have the time, resources, and know-how to care for Reggie in a way that we never could.

The false start with Reggie made us question whether getting a dog was a mistake. Maybe we'd grown too selfish, too set in our routines to make room in our lives for another creature. Or maybe we'd forgotten just how lively Setters can be. Or, more likely, the intervening years since Rebel passed had drained our batteries. Regardless, Reggie was clearly too much dog for us. If we were ever going to try this adoption thing again—and we were by no means certain that we would—the next dog would have to be medium-sized, and with less energy.

Our experience with Reggie wasn't a total loss. His brief time with us taught me a painful lesson about the futility of trying to recapture the past: you really can't go home again. In my quest for the "perfect" dog, I'd gotten what I wanted, but not what I needed. That would come next, and it wouldn't be pretty.

# PET INSURANCE: Luxury Or Necessity?

The cost of Reggie's treatment was a major factor in our decision to return him to the rescue organization. Thankfully, he was adopted by a veterinarian who could absorb the cost his medical care.

In the past, dogs and cats were regarded as property and little consideration was given to their health. That has changed. The majority of pet owners now consider their four-legged friends to be family members. When their pets fall ill or suffer an accident, they're willing to shell out big money—an estimated $14 billion dollars in 2013—for MRIs, radiation, chemotherapy, surgical procedures and other complex treatments that were once the province of human medicine. This year, it's estimated that as many as one in three of America's 78 million pet dogs will require unforeseen vet care, yet less than 1% of them are covered by insurance. While pet insurance isn't a panacea, it can offer some protection in the event of a catastrophic illness or accident.

**Before Buying Pet Insurance**

- ✓ Shop several companies to compare prices, coverage and exclusions. Like human insurance, pet policies have deductibles, co-pays, and caps that can limit payments by incident, illness or calendar year. Most pet policies are subject to exclusions for preexisting conditions and surcharges for older animals and those with chronic conditions.

- ✓ Check to see if the companies you are considering are registered with your state's regulatory agencies or have complaints against them with the department of consumer affairs of the Better Business Bureau.
- ✓ Investigate the financial health of the company underwriting the policy. You want it to still be solvent if, and, more likely, when you need it to pony up.
- ✓ Ask your veterinarian which companies he or she recommends and whose coverage they accept.
- ✓ If your local vet doesn't offer 24-hour emergency care, call the closest facility that does and make sure they'll accept the insurance you're thinking of purchasing.
- ✓ Don't neglect preventative care, checkups and good pet nutrition. A healthy dog that is properly restrained is likely to suffer fewer problems and accidents than one that's obese, neglected or allowed to roam free.

**Pet Insurers: United States, Canada & Britain**
- ✓ Pets Best
- ✓ TruPanion
- ✓ Veterinary Pet Insurance (VPI)
- ✓ PetPlan
- ✓ HealthyPaws
- ✓ Embrace Pet Insurance
- ✓ ASPCA
- ✓ Pet First Healthcare
- ✓ Pet Partners
- ✓ Pet Premium

**Resources**

- Dr. Howie Baker, DVM
- Liz Weston, "Should You Buy Pet Insurance?"
- American Veterinary Medical Association
- Gayle B. Roman, "How To Choose The Right Pet Health Insurance"
- PetFinder, "Pet Insurance Myths and Rumors"

# CHAPTER 3
# BACK ON THE HORSE

*Summer, and first grade is behind me. I pretend that I'm glad, like the other kids. But I'm not. I like school; the structure and quiet suit me, and I get straight A's, or whatever they gave back then. My mother's tired and frazzled; her four young kids have too much time to kill and no safe place to run loose. She scrapes together a few bucks and buys a swing set and a small pool "on time" from Sears—a major coup for her. My immigrant grandparents go ballistic. It's bad for the grass, and they love their manicured yard, which reminds them of Italy. My father sides with them; they're his parents, and they also pay his markers with the shylocks. My mother protests. He roughs her up, and takes a hammer to the pool. The swings are gone the next day.*

~~~

**The writer and his wife, Eugenie, with Reggie**

Our tearful goodbye with Reggie left us physically and emotionally spent. The following day, to shake our blues, we drove across the hill to catch a movie in neighboring Westlake Village. As we were leaving the theatre, Eugenie suggested that we check out a dog adoption at the nearby PetCo. I was floored.

In my experience, women are often emotionally tougher than men. They might tolerate our juvenile behavior and even our abuse, but once they resolve to cut ties, the deed is done. Period. By contrast, men will drag out a break-up for months, even years; sometimes out of laziness, often because they can't bring themselves to hurt their partners, even when the relationship has clearly hit the skids. When dumped, a man will often carry a torch for decades, like Bogart's Rick in *Casablanca*.

Reggie had been gone less than a day and my wife was already moving on!

"That's not healthy," I thought. "That's cold. Scary cold."

As if she read my mind, she hastened to add, "We're not ready to do anything, but looking might help shift our mood, kind of like getting back on the horse after you've been tossed."

Relieved that I hadn't married Lucrezia Borgia, I agreed to take a look. As we stood there eyeballing the ragtag collection of sad, abandoned pets, none of them particularly handsome or charismatic, I couldn't imagine finding a dog to compare with the beautiful but damaged specimen that we'd just surrendered. Eugenie assured me that she understood. We'd just keep looking until we did find one. But I was in no mood for consolation. To underline the futility of our search, I suggested that we drop by the L.A. County Shelter in Agoura Hills, which we had to pass on the way home.

As we entered the building, a young volunteer was kenneling a newly surrendered dog, some kind of a Spaniel. His muzzle was gray, his eyes cloudy, his gait uneven. Had his owners died? Or had the crushing recession forced them to abandon their four-legged charge, leaving him to face his end with strangers? Unbalanced by the newcomer's energy, the "residents" went berserk, pacing, jumping, and barking frantically. All except one muscular brown dog that lay curled up on his threadbare bed, head low, eyes averted.

According to the intake sheet, "Tanner" was a stray Pit Bull mix, approximately two-years-old. He'd been found wandering on Pacific Coast Highway near Oxnard on February 24, the day that we first got Reggie. He was withdrawn and underweight which exaggerated his massive head. Maybe I felt sorry for him. Or maybe a part of me liked the idea of having a badass Pit bull. Or maybe it was just his timid demeanor, so completely opposite that of the super charged Setter. *Something* about the sad, shy dog called out to me. We told the volunteers that we'd think about him. Then we left and drove home.

We had a while to kick it around. In two days' time we were starting a kitchen makeover. Our condo complex had been built nearly forty years before, to offer city dwellers an affordable beach escape. The construction was slap-dash: moldings were crooked, windows out of whack, outlets and fixtures dangerously lacking in electrical tape and safe connectors. There was no insulation. The patio sliders had been installed backwards. It seemed like the builder's mantra had been "Spare every expense!" Despite the shoddy workmanship, however, values had soared on the rising tide of the housing bubble. Weekend crash pads were now pricey, full-time homes.

Except for paint and new appliances, our own kitchen had gone untouched since day one. The tile counters were stained and cracked, the dingy, fiberboard cabinets warped and sagging. The globe lighting screamed Nixon and Watergate. When a newspaper ad promised a quickie remodel for under five grand, we'd jumped at the chance. That was before Reggie. Now, with all of the noise, mess, and stress that the project would entail, there was no way we would dare toss a frightened, abused Pit bull into the mix.

~~~

By the end of the first day the walls had been gutted and the fridge was parked in the center of the living room. All four levels of the condo were coated in fine white dust, like a modern day Pompeii. The Chinese installers spoke no English. Every misstep—a botched oven cutout, a cracked granite slab, some missing floor tiles—meant dozens of frantic calls to their boss who assured me each time that it would all be okay.

By week's end a kitchen emerged, miraculously, from the rubble. New wood cabinets had been hung, granite counters were in, and my daily shout-outs with the headman had dropped to single digits. We were free to think about dogs again.

For twenty years I have taught karate at a friend's dojo in Thousand Oaks, a town just a short drive from the Agoura Shelter. On my way to class that week I stopped by to check on Tanner. I stood by the pen, gently calling his name. As before, he kept to his bed. He seemed less frightened but still wary of human contact. This second meeting confirmed my initial impression: I really liked him. Eugenie had concerns about the breed's reputation for unprovoked violence, plus the prospect of another failed adoption. So I said goodbye, and vowed to put him out of my mind.

After ten frantic days, the last floor tile was cemented into place. The kitchen was done. To celebrate, we drove to Palm Springs to visit Eugenie's mom. During our stay, we checked out local rescue dogs. None of them moved us. When we returned from the desert, we stopped by the beautiful new County facility in West Los Angeles where we found several potential candidates. Eugenie favored a small poodle while I was drawn to a sturdy-looking

Shepherd-mix. All the while, the image of Tanner still hovered in the background of my mind.

Later that week, Eugenie drove across the hill to get her nails done. She came back with disturbing news. She'd gone by the shelter to check on Tanner and had seen a father and son cuddling him inside one of the recreation pens. She didn't stick around but, judging from their interest, she deduced that they would likely adopt him.

I tried to be fatalistic; it would mean a good situation for a neglected dog, and there would still be scores of others for us to consider. But I was disappointed. Obsessed with finding another Setter like Rebel, I'd never even considered having a Pit bull. Now I couldn't get this one out of my head. I was Romeo pledging true love for Rosaline only to kick her to the curb when Juliet sashayed by. I didn't know why (and wouldn't for some time), but it was as if this particular dog and I were meant to be together.

The following Saturday we went back to visit the shelter. To our surprise and relief, Tanner was still there. We spent some time alone with him in the play area. He definitely seemed to be coming out of his shell, no mean feat for a dog in canine prison. And the volunteers all raved about his sweet disposition. After our close call I wanted dibs on him before someone swooped in and stole him away. Eugenie still wasn't totally sold, so she left the decision to me.

For legal reasons, and to protect Tanner, they had us sign a form acknowledging that we were considering adoption of a "dominant breed" dog. We promised that we would treat him humanely with regard to his health and safety, or return him to the shelter if we no longer could. The woman at the desk said that we could expect a decision in four or five days. The die was finally cast. Either Tanner would be ours or we'd have to let him go and find another dog.

~~~

Two days later, on April 13, I was writing in my office when the call came in. Our application had been approved; Tanner was ours! We were elated, and unnerved. Talking about him was one thing. Now he would actually be joining our home. We hoped that he'd be as gentle as he had appeared. But what if he had been playing possum and actually turned out to be a snarling, vicious monster? And what about his health? He seemed sound, but so had Reggie.

To burn off my anxiety, I prepped the condo for his arrival. Like a desperate housewife tweaking crystal meth I bounced around folding clothes, vacuuming rugs, and scrubbing everything in sight. Eugenie watched, dumbstruck, as I balanced on a ladder, dusting ceiling beams that had gone untouched for nearly twenty years. What was I thinking? If the dog could access the rafters, a messy house would be the least of our problems.

We arrived at the shelter shortly before closing. We signed the forms and paid the adoption fee, a mere fifty dollars and change that included shots, micro-chipping, and a free vet visit—maybe the best bargain since the Dutch bought Manhattan. We were told to go to the kennel area where volunteers would bring us our dog.

**Tanner**

# "DOMINANT" BREEDS & PIT BULLS

In Los Angeles County, "dominant" breeds include Pit bulls, Rottweilers, Staffordshire Bull Terriers, American Staffordshire Terriers, Mastiffs, Chow Chows, Jindos, Shar Peis, Dogo Argentino, Cane Corso, Presa Canario and any breed with a history of fighting.

The term *Pit Bull* commonly refers to the American Pit Bull Terrier, American Staffordshire Terrier, Staffordshire Bull Terrier, or any other dog that has similar physical characteristics and appearance. These breeds take their roots from the Bulldog and various terriers. The American Kennel Club describes the American Staffordshire Terrier as "...a people-oriented dog that thrives when he is made part of the family and given a job to do. Although friendly, this breed is loyal to his family and will protect them from any threat. His short coat is low-maintenance, but regular exercise and training is necessary."

Petey, the white and black dog featured on *The Little Rascals* and *Our Gang* comedies was a Pit Bull.

**Resources**

- The American Kennel Club

# CHAPTER 4
# A VERY ANGRY GUY

*I'm twelve and terrified, slinking down the sidewalk, trying hard to be invisible. Neat trick for a tall, blubbery boy (in the PC-speak of the 60s they call us "husky") with thick black Clark Kent glasses. The fifty yards from the school door to my house feels like fifty miles, with the sinewy Irish punk who's lurking on the corner looking to kick my ass.*

*I slip by somehow and make it home, but she's waiting by the window, determined I stop running and face my bogeyman. I plead to deaf ears. My mother drags me outside to the front lawn, calls him over and demands that we "settle it. Now!"*

*The tough kid's as unnerved as I am, but we do as we're told, pushing, shoving, and flailing clumsily.*

*As we roll around in the grass, my glasses break. Suddenly I tap into something strange, something raw and hot, a piece of me that I didn't know existed. I body slam that Irish kid and pin his arms until he "gives." My mom sends me back inside. She doesn't know it—I don't either—but the genie is out of the bottle.*

***The writer and his father, 1952***

Every morning, before the alarm detonates, Eugenie wiggles over to my side of the bed and burrows into my arms. It's a ritual that we began when we left New York, where we were always "too busy" for silly things like cuddling. We find that it helps to remind us of what's important, and sets the tone for the new day. But things were different now: we had Tanner.

We skipped the spooning, hurried upstairs and unlatched the crate, eager to greet our new baby. Tanner ventured out to meet us, trembling from head to toe. That he was frightened was understandable. For two months the County kennel had been his home; he'd grown used to its sights, sounds, and smells. Then, suddenly, he'd been whisked away to start over again with total strangers. We tried to soothe him with praise and affection. That only seemed to worsen his anxiety.

I'm a zombie without my coffee, but I threw on shoes and rushed him outside. We hiked the property for thirty minutes, waiting for him to "go." When he finally emptied his bowels, I carried on like he'd just pulled a dozen children from a burning orphanage. Thankfully, there was no one around to watch my victory dance. 6:00 AM was too early for sane people to be out and about.

~~~

Back before Rebel and Eugenie, when I worked in the New York club scene, we didn't close until 4:00 AM. Afterwards, my buddies and I would head out for breakfast, or grab a nightcap at one of the seedy after-hours dives that existed in droves back then. To sugarcoat our debauchery we told ourselves, as long as we were asleep by sunrise, we were still "normal." Like Mark Twain said, "Denial ain't just a river in Egypt."

The incident that spurred me to clean up my act took place on the eve of a funeral. My mother's sister had succumbed to a long illness. The burial was scheduled for 9:00 AM the following day in Bayonne, NJ. To ensure that I'd be on time, I borrowed my sister's car and parked it in front of my building. Tow away would start at 8:00, but I'd be gone by then since the drive to Jersey would take an hour.

I left work early that night but instead of going home I met a girlfriend for a drink. The drink turned into a party at my place. Sometime around 5:00 A.M. I tucked her into a cab, then I crawled back inside to catch a few hours' rest.

I woke in a panic. The alarm was blaring. My head was pounding. Sunlight was flooding the apartment. The clock read 8:25. Shielding my glazed eyes I glanced out the window. On the street below, a City tow truck was hooking up the car behind the one I'd borrowed. I snatched my wrinkled clothes from the chair. Fueled by desperation and an epic surge of adrenalin I blasted down seven flights of stairs, past the dumbfounded doorman, out onto West 4$^{th}$ Street. As the tow truck pulled up next to my ride, I slid behind the wheel, cranked the engine, and peeled out.

Changing as I drove, I reached the funeral home at 9:30. The procession had already left. I scribbled down directions to the cemetery and roared off again. When I pulled into the graveyard, my mother and siblings were already exiting their cars. I'd concocted a shameless alibi (a rogue power outage?) to explain my absence and bizarre appearance. Their icy stares cut me off; I was a derelict sleazebag, deserving of no pity. I made it through that day, one of the longest of my life, and quit the club biz for the ascetic life of a cabbie. Now I was up before dawn, walking my dog.

~~~

When we got back from our walk, Eugenie broke out Rebel's old dish, filled it with kibble, and set it on the floor. Tanner stayed glued to his bed. We took our coffee and retreated to the dining room table. Once the coast was clear, he got up and, keeping as far from us as possible, carefully inched his way to the food. He ate in fits and starts, casting fearful glances over his shoulder as if we might attack him.

It was like that for the entire week. Noises or sudden movements—a dropped newspaper, a rattled plate—sent Tanner flying across the room. The mere sight of the car plunged him into a panic: he dug in his heels like a condemned man being dragged to the gallows. If we went for a ride, even to the corner, he blew his lunch. Each time that he emptied his stomach I could feel my jaw clench and my temperature rise.

Tanner was scared of practically everything. He was also housebroken and didn't beg, bark, or jump on the furniture. Someone had taken the time to teach him the basics. But his fearful demeanor and some nasty scars suggested that his manners had come at a price. Whatever happened to him before the shelter, it probably wasn't good.

It took a week before the quaking and wincing stopped. The sun was already sitting on the ocean one morning when we unlocked the kennel door. Tanner bolted out to greet us. Tail wagging, he belly-crawled across the loft, legs splayed out behind him. It was a freakish display of agility for such a muscular dog, and the first tiny sign of progress.

After that, I couldn't wait for our morning reunions. Careful not to wake Eugenie, I'd slip out of bed and sneak upstairs to watch Tanner sleeping in his kennel. It was my secret pleasure, sitting there listening to his gentle breathing, watching his muscular, tan and white chest rise and fall.

When he woke, I'd set him free. Then we'd start our rituals. There'd be belly crawling, rump rubbing (his, not mine), yoga (of course, downward dog is his favorite pose) and some frisky doggie kisses. If I wasn't knocked cold (his skull's the size of a cinder block and just as hard), we'd set off on our walk.

Shelter dogs don't get much leash time; the staff and volunteers are swamped just caring for their basic needs. Despite that, Tanner didn't balk or pull when I walked him. He also didn't mark the territory, a sure sign that, for him at least, this new arrangement was by no means permanent.

It was during one of these early morning jaunts that he made his first friend, an aged Retriever named Shiloh. I didn't tell Eugenie, but I was anxious about Tanner and how he might react with other dogs now that he was no longer incarcerated. He and Shiloh sniffed and wagged a brief hello, then moved on like they'd been pals for years. It was a perfect meeting between an old, relaxed dog and a young, uncertain one. Watching Shiloh stagger off I couldn't help thinking that, all too soon, Tanner would be the rheumy-eyed graybeard welcoming some upstart young stud to his 'hood.

If, as scientists believe, dogs have no sense of their own mortality, aging must be very strange for them. They must wonder why the walks keep getting longer, why the squirrels keep getting faster, and why their people keep raising the sofa and bed.

~~~

Because we don't have children, friends showered us with "baby gifts" to welcome the new addition. There were chew sticks, fancy liver treats, and a basket of toys that included a skinny blue Dachshund and stretchy Shar Pei from my sister, Honey, a lieutenant in the Hudson County (NJ) Prosecutor's office. Honey's tough on dirt bags but she's a total mush where kids and animals are concerned. She has had a slew of big, kooky rescue dogs—Huskies, Samoyeds, Rottweilers—and spoiled them all. She was clearly aiming to do the same with Tanner.

We sorted through the loot and weeded out the pull-toys. Tug of war can be fun. It can also encourage aggressive, dominant behavior. As a Pit Bull, Tanner already had two strikes against him. What if he lunged for a toy and accidentally seized some youngster's hand with those powerful jaws? Better to play it safe and stick with fetch.

~~~

I dangled the plush Shar Pei in front of Tanner.

"Look at this!" I cooed in my most excited dog voice.

Tanner crept up warily and brushed it with his snout. To fan his interest, I pinched the squeaker. He jumped and bolted back to his bed. Eugenie and I were stunned. Who ever heard of a dog that didn't like squeaky toys!

Pit Bulls are terriers, and terriers are known for their stubborn (obsessive?) temperaments. Try shooing a Jack Russell away from a gopher hole, or prying a tennis ball from the vise-grip mouth of a Bull Terrier. But I can be relentless, too. I was determined to see Tanner play like a normal dog.

I collected the stuffed toy and let fly. Tanner didn't budge. I retrieved it and heaved again. And again. And again. Finally, on what felt like the thousandth throw, he popped up, sped across the floor, launched himself in the air, and pounced, seizing "Sharpie" in his bear trap maw. Eugenie and I cheered like he'd taken Best In Show at Westminster. Arm dangling limply, I strode across the room and gently demanded that he "give" me the toy. I half-expected him to chew off my fingers. Instead, he meekly surrendered his cuddly prey.

Squeaky toys spooked him. Treats were a different ballgame. We'd planned on saving the liver bits for special occasions. Tanner wasn't having it. He blocked our path to the fridge, balanced on his hind legs, and stuck out his paw. Suckers that we are, it worked like a charm and left us wondering what other tricks the little hustler had in store.

On karate nights, I would usually stick around after class, discussing martial arts techniques or philosophy with the students. Now I hurried home to join my sweetheart and my wife for cuddles. At bedtime, Eugenie suggested letting Tanner walk himself into the crate instead of *helping* him like we'd been doing. Why not? This wasn't Reggie, who had to be wrestled down and dragged inside. When we entered the loft she fished out some treats and tossed them into the kennel.

"Come to bed," she purred.

Tanner dutifully trotted over. He snaked his snout through the door, hoovered up the snacks, and lit out for the stairs. He was fast. I was faster. I cut him off, slipped the collar over his bowling ball dome, and hauled him back to his bunk. So much for allowing.

~~~

I'm a sound sleeper. I've dozed through countless cacophonous New York nights and a dozen earthquakes, including the giant Northridge shaker, but Tanner's muted cries woke me before dawn. Shelter dogs are walked and fed early, so I presumed the whining was his way of telling me to get cracking and tend to his needs. I wasn't about to let a pushy newcomer dictate my sleep schedule; that's Eugenie's job. I tiptoed out of the room, "sshed" him, and went back to bed, pleased that I'd nipped the rebellion in the bud.

Turned out he wasn't being bossy; the dog was starving. While fixing breakfast, Eugenie discovered that she'd misread the guidelines. Instead of the recommended three cups of kibble per day, Tanner had been getting a mere three scoops, about six ounces! No wonder he was complaining and looking stressed. Between the car vomiting and accidental starvation, the shelter—with its dull routine and regular, plentiful meals—must have seemed like paradise.

Toward the end of that first week, we took him to the vet for his official post-adoption exam. As we waited to see the doctor, we assured ourselves that what had happened with Reggie was a freak occurrence. That Tanner would check out just fine. Secretly, though, we feared that the rescue gods might frown on us again. If they did, at least this time we would know before we grew attached.

Only one month earlier Dr. Lisa had performed the fateful exam on Reggie. She'd needed a muzzle and a strapping attendant to subdue the ailing Setter. Tanner didn't flail or fuss. He wagged his tail and stood calmly while she poked and prodded. She pronounced him in great health and possessed of a sweet temperament, a huge improvement over his rambunctious predecessor.

He topped the scales at fifty pounds. The vet guessed him to be younger than the shelter estimate, somewhere between 12-16 months—basically a large, muscular puppy. She also confirmed what we'd suspected; that he was all Pit Bull and not a "mix," at all, the designation used by shelters to make dominant-breed dogs more adoptable.

To celebrate his clean bill of health we drove to Santa Monica for lunch at our favorite Italian deli. As usual, the place was mobbed. The cramped parking lot was overflowing. After some fancy wrangling I finally managed to snag a space. Just as we were pulling in, Tanner yawned and tossed up his breakfast.

"Son-of-a-bitch!" I growled, pounding the steering wheel in frustration. "What's wrong with this dog!"

Eugenie jabbed me with her elbow. "Calm down," she said. Her voice was soft but there was iron in it. "You're scaring him."

She nodded toward the back seat where Tanner lay cringing. Instead of turkey and provolone heroes, I drove to the nearest gas station and mopped up another pile of gooey kibble.

Back home, I cleaned and disinfected the seat covers and upholstery. I called Dr. Lisa, who suggested we try drugs to curb Tanner's motion sickness. I was so grossed out that I'd have tried Krazy Glue. Even worse than the vomiting, though, was my ugly response and Tanner's reaction to it. He'd been with us less than a week and he'd already sniffed out the dark secret I'd worked most of my life to deny: that I was one very angry guy.

~~~

I used to say that I inherited my fiery nature from my father. His formal education ended with junior high school, but he had a razor sharp mind, especially when it came to devising schemes to boost his income or calculate the odds at a craps table. A charming, hotheaded restaurateur and compulsive gambler, he used anger and intimidation to silence anyone foolish enough to challenge him. He rarely hit his children but the message that he modeled for us was clear: be loud enough and menacing enough and the world will bend to your will. He died of a massive heart attack at the age of sixty-eight, arguing with a customer at the family restaurant.

Twenty-five years later, I was following in his footsteps. I didn't brawl in the street, kick the cat, or beat my wife. And, to friends and acquaintances, I seemed calm and controlled. Yet, despite therapy, meditation, and three decades of martial arts, I had a reservoir of rage simmering inside me, just below the surface, waiting for any excuse to erupt. Even something as trivial as a turkey sandwich.

~~~

*A sultry August day early in our courtship. To escape the blast furnace city heat, Eugenie and I take the Long Island Railroad from Penn Station to Jones Beach.*

*An hour shvitzing in the sun, and we're starving. She stays behind, guarding our spot, while I trek a mile of fiery sand to the food concession. Eugenie wants a burger. I order turkey on rye. I emphatically request "No mayo." The product of an Italian household where butter, olive oil and vinegar were the only condiments, the texture of mayonnaise creeps me out.*

*An hour later, I slog back to our blanket. I unwrap my lunch, and what do I find? "You mother————!" I throw down the sandwich in disgust. Stomping it maniacally, I boot it down the beach, barely missing a pair of hulking bodybuilders. I never litter, so I collect the flattened roll and heave it in the trash. I make my way back to Eugenie. She hasn't bailed, but her crimson-tinged face is buried in a book. She's seen enough of "Taxi Driver" in a swimsuit.*

~~~

**Tanner with his "babies"**

The image of Tanner quaking in fear upset me. It also brought a flash of clarity. I suddenly knew that I'd been kidding myself. My fury wasn't an inheritance, the result of some incontrovertible, unalterable DNA. It was a habit that I'd created and allowed to fester, an insidious addiction that cast a pall over what should have been a joyous life, causing sadness for people that I claimed to love. However it may have started, this roiling anger had become my default mode. It defined me.

~~~

My wife and I are polar opposites, at least on the surface. Eugenie is shy, soft-spoken and rarely angry; I'm outgoing, noisy and easily pissed off. She does yoga; I practice karate. She studies Kabbalah and Science of Mind; I read Mishima and *The Art of War*.

Despite our seeming differences, she claims that the moment she saw Scorsese's *Raging Bull*, she knew that the man she was supposed to marry (me) was waiting for her in New York.

After graduating from Stephen's College in Missouri, she lit out for Gotham with a couple thousand in savings and a single letter of recommendation. Like so many greenhorns, the Big Apple gave her a rough welcome. During her first year she bounced around from apartment to apartment (by her count, thirteen in ten months), and job to job, including a very brief stint at *High Society*, a risqué men's magazine that she mistook for a patrician cultural journal. She was down to her last five dollars when a graphic artist she met at a party helped her to land a job as an art director, a position for which she had not a shred of training. Undaunted, she took the gig and prospered, learning as she went.

We met at the gym, introduced by a mutual friend, a striking girl named Debbie. After the introduction, Eugenie and Debbie began to invite me along for movies, concerts, and other social events. Man-slut intuition said that one of these knockouts was casing me, but which one? My dance card was full, so I decided to hold off until my admirer tipped her hand. Then my dad died, and I left New York to be with my mom and siblings.

There's a scene in *The Godfather* where Don Corleone warns his son, Michael, about a pending betrayal from inside the family. He predicts that one of their trusted capos will signal his duplicity by offering to set a meeting with the rival boss, who will then try to have Michael assassinated. I'd been AWOL for two weeks when Eugenie phoned to ask whether I was okay. I explained the situation and thanked her for her concern. When I returned to the City, I took her to a movie, sans Debbie.

After the show, we stopped by my place to take Rebel for a walk. He was excited to have her company. As we waited by the elevator, he wrapped the leash around us, pressing us close together. It was a cute but awkward moment. To ease the tension, I jokingly asked if Eugenie had a curfew. It was an odd question to pose to a grown woman and potential lover. It prompted an even stranger reply.

"Actually, I *am* living with someone, so maybe I should get going."

After all her mating gymnastics, the little minx was taken!

I left Rebel with the doorman and hailed a taxi. As I shut the door, Eugenie sheepishly asked if we could "still be friends."

"Yes," I told her and meant it; unlike dates, good friends were in short supply. I paid the cabbie and sent her on her way. I figured that that was that; the player had gotten played.

A few days later she called to tell me that she was now available. She explained that her old boyfriend had wormed his way into her apartment. When their romance soured, he became abusive and refused to leave. After our platonic date, he roughed her up again. This time she threatened to tell the cops, and he finally cleared out, leaving us free to take our "friendship" to the next level.

Our courtship was easy and fun; it had none of the high drama that had infused my previous relationships. For Eugenie, it was love at first sight. She freely admits that she would have married me in a week. I liked her, too. She was sweet, sexy, and funny but I'd run through a slew of girlfriends over the previous few years. If form held true, and it was way too soon to predict otherwise, she would end up being just another ex.

There was one other minor problem. Having witnessed my parents' trench warfare, the mere notion of "Till death do us part" seemed like torture. For me, anything was preferable to being trapped in a caustic, loveless relationship. It took five years, several breakups, and countless hours of counseling before I was able to set aside my fears and see Eugenie for the gem that she is. Thankfully, she stuck by me until I did.

Open-minded, inquisitive, and always in search of the Big Answers, Eugenie had tackled *A Course in Miracles* (aka The Course, or ACIM) several times, slogging through the stilted 1,200-page text on her own, or in a class at some holistic center. When she learned that friends were hosting a weekly meeting here in Malibu, she wrangled an invitation.

The group meets Tuesday evenings at "The Farm," our friends' place in Serra Retreat, an exclusive enclave that is home to numerous celebrities. For the better part of two decades I'd spent my Tuesdays teaching Okinawan GoJu, the "wax on, wax off" fighting style featured in the original *Karate Kid* movies. Convinced that I'd never ditch karate for something as "groovy" as The Course, Eugenie never broached the subject. She did, however, discuss the lessons, which frequently dealt with anger and forgiveness. Sometimes, after a particularly resonant class, she would say, "Too bad you weren't there; I think you'd have enjoyed it." Now that we had timorous Tanner, I secretly wondered if maybe I shouldn't give it a look.

Back when we first met I'd have scoffed at anything New Age or touchy-feely. As a street-smart black belt from a *Goodfellas* family, I was a take-no-crap, take-no-prisoners wise-ass, and proud of it. Like Cyrano De Bergerac, I savored conflict, and there was plenty to be had in *you-wanna-piece-of-me?* New York. Everywhere we went—the Post Office, the market, the dry cleaners—it seemed like there was always some jerk that needed wising up. I was happy to oblige. I considered it my duty, my karma.

When I wasn't busy trading barbs with strangers, I was serving up heated, caustic rants about art, sports, and politics to friends and acquaintances. Under the guise of honesty I threw words like punches. I was resentful, quarrelsome, negative and mean. I was that "jerk."

In rare lucid moments I had made some reflexive stabs at change. In my late teens I unconsciously gravitated to the martial arts, which helped instill in me a modicum of impulse control that probably spared me from jail or worse. Before then, high school basketball had served as the safety valve for my volatile temper. When college hoops proved unlikely (a triple threat, I was a short, slow, and white), I focused on my studies. I was playing h-o-r-s-e in the gym when a fellow student asked me to join the Karate Club. My freshman grades were perfect but my volcanic energy needed an outlet. I said yes, and soon found myself enthralled with the focus and discipline that the art demanded. While a competitive spirit was essential to martial arts, unbridled emotion was frowned upon. I soon learned that an angry fighter was a vulnerable fighter.

Later, when heated outbursts threatened to derail my romance with Eugenie, I found a counselor who taught me how to communicate in a more evenhanded, less threatening fashion. A savvy veteran of the "couples wars," Judy began our initial session by declaring that our relationship was DOA, that we should quit wasting time and formulate a plan for splitting up. Her grim prognosis had the desired effect: it left us determined to prove her wrong.

We slogged through two years of heated therapy before Judy managed to convince us that our relationship issues—Eugenie's fear of abandonment and my dread of commitment—were not so cut and dry as we believed. We weren't bound to repeat our parents' romantic miscues; we were free to make our own.

In both those instances I had focused on treating the symptoms, not the root cause, by addressing a specific situation, not the underlying problem. Now, thanks to Tanner, I'd reached the end of my irate rope. He'd had a hard young life and deserved a loving, peaceful home. For this dog to blossom and truly feel safe, I'd have to do more than merely modify my behavior: I'd have to change my Self in a fundamental way. Trouble was, I had no clue where to start.

I asked my Sensei if he'd mind shifting my class to another night so I might attend a "philosophy" seminar. He was happy to oblige. When I broke the news to her, Eugenie nearly fainted. She was thrilled, of course, and quickly got permission for Tanner to come along.

~~~

Class began with a brief meditation. When the gong sounded, Tanner settled in beside us and quickly drifted off to sleep. We nudged each other and smiled smugly; he'd been with us only a few days and already his behavior was impeccable. Our pride was short lived, however. He started to snore like a jackhammer, and continued for the rest of the session.

The imposing ACIM tome resembles an old-school Bible, divided into Text, Workbook and Teacher's Manual. Like a karate sensei with a class of senior students, our teacher, Ed, tailors each session to the evolving needs of the group. On my first evening there, he opted to revisit one of the early workbook lessons: *"I Am Determined To See Things Differently."* The exercise was clear and simple: identify any and all people, behavior, and situations that make us angry, regardless of how seemingly trivial, and resolve to see them in a new, more peaceful light.

I was taken aback. It was as if he'd chosen the topic especially for me. Of course, given the breadth and volume of the things that pissed me off, from political malfeasance to pineapple pizza, I'd be dead before I ever made a dent.

I followed the discussion as best I could and left feeling guardedly hopeful. If this approach worked—and a roomful of intelligent people attested that it did—there just might be a way to exorcise my rage and heal my dog.

*Tanner*

# *PREVENTING DOG AGGRESSION*

**Signs of Dog Aggression**
- ✓ Growling, teeth bared, muzzle wrinkled.
- ✓ Intense stare, tense facial expression.
- ✓ Head held high, ears up and forward. Flattened ears can signal a fearful dog.
- ✓ Tail high and stiff, either with no movement, or flagging rapidly back and forth. A tucked tail often means a dog is scared.
- ✓ Hair on back raised.
- ✓ Posture alert and intense, chest and head up, weight forward, attempting to seem as big and threatening as possible. Frightened dogs will often cower or crouch.

**Reasons For Aggressive Behavior**
- ✓ <u>Dominance</u>: A dog may show aggression to establish dominance over other animals and, sometimes, even humans.
- ✓ <u>Territory</u>: Aggressive behavior may be an attempt to claim or defend its perceived territory, like the feeding area, the back yard, or its owner's bed.
- ✓ <u>Fear</u>: A fearful dog may resort to aggressive behavior to protect itself from perceived threats. This can be an issue with shelter dogs, many of which were abused and mistreated.

- ✓ Medical Problems: Sick or injured dogs and pregnant or nursing females might lash out when they feel threatened or cornered.
- ✓ Instinct: Dogs with a strong prey drive can view children, small dogs, and cats as prey.

**Dog Bites—Some Numbers**
- ▶ According to the Center for Disease Control, approximately 4.5 million Americans suffer dog bites each year. 1-in-5 dog bites will require medical attention.
- ▶ In a survey of dog bite fatalities from 1979 through 1998 at least 30 breeds, including Pit Bulls, Rottweilers, German Shepherds, Huskies, Alaskan Malamutes, Doberman Pinschers, Chows, Great Danes, St. Bernards, and Akitas were implicated.
- ▶ While "dominant" breed dogs are responsible for the vast majority of dog bite deaths, in October 2000 a 6-week-old Los Angeles baby was killed by her family's 4-lb. Pomeranian.

**Curbing Dog Aggression**
- ✓ Before buying or adopting a dog, ask a professional—a trainer, vet or breeder—which breeds make sense for your family situation.
- ✓ With rescue dogs, ask if the shelter staff performed a behavioral assessment. How did the dog respond to

other dogs? When people took away its food? To rough petting of the kind children might dish out?

- ✓ Spend time with the dog before bringing it home. If possible, train and socialize your dog before introducing it into your home. According to veteran trainer Tony Rollins, it can take 90 days for a shelter dog to "come back" to its true nature. For that reason, it's best to get help from a professional who can assess your dog's personality and teach you how to avoid future problems.
- ✓ Spay or neuter your dog. In addition to preventing overpopulation, this can reduce aggressive behavior.
- ✓ Avoid wrestling with your dog until you've bonded with him. A dog can view rough play as a contest for supremacy. Your dog sees tug-of-war a pack effort to "kill" the "prey" (the tug toy). You can always play fetch or catch with a Frisbee, which fosters a form of pack responsiveness. When playing tug-of-war, it's important to establish rules like "give." If you are unsure about these activities, consult a professional.
- ✓ From the start, practice taking away your dog's food and toys. You should be able put your hand near the dog while he's eating without him reacting aggressively.
- ✓ Do not let a dog with aggressive tendencies on the furniture, especially your bed. Aggressive male dogs may try to protect a female owner from her mate, and vice versa.

- ✓ Do not hit, scream at, or otherwise abuse your dog since these behaviors can frighten him, increasing the likelihood of aggression.
- ✓ Education is more important and more effective than punishment. It's unfair to punish a dog for something he hasn't been properly taught. Humans are automatically the pack leaders since they control the resources. Gandhi and Stalin were both pack leaders. One led by example and inspiration, the other by force and fear. Which kind do you want to be?
- ✓ If your dog displays aggressive tendencies, seek immediate professional assistance.

**Dog Safety Rules For Children:**
- ✓ Never approach a strange dog.
- ✓ Never run from a dog, shout, or scream.
- ✓ If a strange dog approaches you, stand still. If knocked down, roll into a ball and be still.
- ✓ Never play with dogs unless supervised by an adult.
- ✓ Avoid making eye contact with dogs.
- ✓ Before petting a dog, ask permission from the owner and always let the dog see and sniff you first.
- ✓ Never bother a dog that is sleeping, eating, or caring for puppies.

**Resources**

- Centers for Disease Control
- *Los Angeles Times*
- Sacks JJ, Sinclair L, Gilchrist J, Golab GC, Lockwood R. "Breeds of dogs involved in fatal human attacks in the U.S. between 1979 and 1998." *JAVMA (Journal of the American Veterinary Medical Association)*, 2000; 217:836-840
- Tony Rollins, Tony Rollins K-9 Academy
- Rob Lerner, CPDT-KA
- ASPCA
- Dr. Howie Baker, DVM

# CHAPTER 5
# "FIRST" THINGS FIRST

On the street outside, car doors slam. The front door swings open and in they huff, my father's sister, Tess, and his brothers, Mike and Junior, both respected doctors. Tightlipped, they head downstairs to my grandparents' flat.

It's not a birthday, or a name day, or their anniversary, so their presence and the strained voices mean something big is up. The "something" is my father, in hock up to his eyeballs again, hoping they'll step in and square things with the "shys", his pals the loan sharks.

"It's done! No more! Finished!" They take turns screaming, cursing, pleading for him to get help with his "sickness"—an Italian intervention. "Let them break my legs, or kill me," he says, dismissing their concern. "I really don't give a damn!" He bulls out, indignant, daring them to stick to their guns and shoot the hostage, to hold him accountable. They won't. They'll make good like last time, and all the times before. And he knows it. Listening to their ranting and raging should scare us but we shrug it off. In our house, it's business as usual.

**Tanner's first trip to the beach**

We'd put our normal routines on hold and had been hanging around the house for some weeks, helping Tanner adjust to his new digs. But now it was time to get back to work. I'm a writer and my wife's a stone sculptor. Because we're fond of food, electricity and running water, we also moonlight as personal trainers.

It's fun to exercise and help people stay healthy, but the job has its drawbacks. Schedules change from week to week. Client vacations wreak havoc with cash flow. And there's no benefits package. On the plus side—and it's a huge plus—we've become friends with many of our clients who graciously share their lives and homes with us. For Tanner to mesh with our freewheeling lifestyle he would have to get used to the car. If not, we'd be forced to leave him behind, which we didn't want to do until he'd grown more comfortable with us.

Eugenie was sculpting at the stone yard when the drug store called to say that Tanner's anti-nausea meds were ready. I was caught between a rock and a barf place. I could leave him alone to demolish the house or bring him along and have him hurl in the car. I'd had my fill of upchuck. I sped to the pharmacy, cut to the head of the line, grabbed the drugs, and raced home.

I entered the condo prepared for Armageddon; Reggie had been tall enough to reach nearly everything in the house and hyper enough to try. I found Tanner where I'd left him, stretched out beside my desk, his big, brown eyes alert for any hint of displeasure.

To reward him for not ransacking the place we took a walk to the pool where we ran into our neighbors, Hiroshi and Bonnie, and their Boston Terrier, Winnie.

We owed our friendship with them to another dog, my mother-in-law's Pug, Dudley. Eugenie's mom, Melissa, lives in Palm Springs where summer temperatures often top 100 degrees. It's unpleasant for most dogs, but especially so for short-snouted (brachiocephalic) dogs like Shih Tzu, Pekinese, Boston Terriers, French Bulldogs, and Pugs. To escape the brutal heat, she'd pack Dudley off to stay with us at the beach. During one of Dud's vacations he introduced himself to Winnie and they hit it off. From then on, whenever he came to visit, we'd rendezvous in the evenings to walk together. While we humans railed about politics or the failings of our homeowners association, our push-faced dogs would trot side-by-side, ignoring each other like an old married couple.

Pit Bulls aren't Pugs. Not even close. Tanner lunged at Winnie, who backpedaled furiously, snarling like a dingo. Here was a lady who disliked the direct approach. Tanner skidded to a halt, stung. Couldn't she see how cute he was? He stretched out on his stomach, groaning passionately, begging her to reconsider. Winnie curled her lip; she still wasn't having it. I felt sorry to see Tanner so forlorn, but I was also relieved. So far he'd met several dogs of different sizes and temperaments, and had been playful and submissive with them all. If there were psycho, homicidal Pit Bulls running amok out there, Tanner wasn't one of them.

The next morning I slipped some meclizine-laced ham in with his kibble. Then we drove to Malibu Colony for a workout with longtime clients, Carl and Roberta, who host the Course In Miracles. The Colony is built on the remnants of a 17,000-acre Rancho owned by the Rindge Family, just west of the Malibu Pier; it boasts 100+ multimillion-dollar homes squeezed together like Philly row houses on a half-mile tract of some of the world's most coveted sand. In the 1940s, when financial problems forced the last heir to sell, lots could be had for $6,500. Now, summer rentals *start* at $50,000 a month.

Carl and Charlie, their Cavalier King Charles, were waiting in the courtyard of the beachfront cottage. Despite his size, Charlie is an alpha male. His first reaction was to mount the newcomer. Some dogs aren't keen on being violated. Tanner didn't care. He just sat down and waited patiently until his new friend tired of humping air.

Instead of warming up on the treadmill, the four of us jogged to the end of the private road where we caught a glimpse of Sting doing Pilates with his trainer. It was Tanner's first celebrity sighting. He wasn't impressed, and later confided that he prefers hip hop, especially Snoop Dogg.

His nonchalance was typical for *The 'Bu*, where ordinary folks take great pains to act blasé in the presence of our rich and famous neighbors. Maybe we're jaded or jealous, but no self-respecting Malibuite would ever think of interrupting a star's dinner to gush or beg an autograph. Just the opposite. Like Greenpeace activists with baby seals, we're protective of our models, moguls, actors, and jocks. We'll block the road in order to rescue a besieged pop star from the media circus, or throw down with paparazzi that invade a favorite surf break to land a "gotcha" picture of Matthew McConaughey.

From platinum-selling rockers and silver screen A-listers to first round castoffs from *Dancing With the Stars*, the same, unwritten rule applies when dealing with celebs: Be cool. Very cool. It's not always easy. One evening shortly after we first moved here, we stopped to grab coffee before a movie. It was raining, and the cafe was empty save for us, the barista, and a pair of muscular men - Sylvester Stallone and his imposing bodyguard. Like old friends from back in the day we casually nodded hello, paid for our lattes, and left to catch the show.

On the way back from Carl's we stopped to check out The Lumber Yard, an upscale shopping center that had recently opened. When we came to Malibu in 1991, the city had an actual lumber yard, plus three hardware stores and dozens of mom and pop retailers selling everything from surfboards to feathered pumps. Nearly all of them have vanished, pushed out by retail chains or uber-chic boutiques that hawk $300 T-shirts, biker bling, and designer eyewear.

We're not the only ones to find the change unsettling. As we parked the car, Tanner dredged up a pile of partially digested breakfast. Choking back curses, I drove to a deserted lot by the Malibu Lagoon where I scraped up another gooey puddle. On the surface I seemed calm but Tanner wasn't fooled. He hung his head and started shaking violently.

~~~

His carsickness (and my temper) aside, Tanner was slowly starting to loosen up and show his true colors. We were out walking one afternoon when a kamikaze squirrel bolted from the bushes and brazenly skittered across our path. Tanner assumed "the position" and froze. Ears up, brow furrowed, chest puffed out, he loosed a primal, guttural cry that stood my hair on end. He might be timid and queasy but his prey drive was still very much alive.

As the daredevil squirrel chattered noisily from the safety of a Ponderosa pine, I dragged Tanner away and started for home. On the sidewalk up ahead, my neighbor, Bettina, and her Lab-mix, Otto, were playing with a neighbor's young daughter. Catching sight of Tanner, Otto stiffened his tail and growled. In doggie-speak he was flipping off the newcomer, telling him to beat it or else. I wondered which Tanner would emerge if I held the course and braved a showdown, the fearful shelter dog that we'd rescued or the darker, instinctive predator that ached to cull the local rodent population?

So far, Tanner seemed docile. I was fairly certain he'd back down but two weeks wasn't time enough to know for sure. Being an outlaw breed, if he wound up in a fight and injured another dog, the blame would fall on him regardless the cause. I teach my karate students that avoidance is the best defense. We crossed the street and trotted home to dinner.

Otto had never met Tanner yet he had acted like they were Crips and Bloods. It left me wondering just why dogs take offense with other dogs? Did Tanner resemble some Pit Bull that had teased him at school or insulted his sister? Or maybe Tanner was too clean and smelled bad? Or perhaps Otto simply didn't like his walk, his coat, the way he carried his tail, or the color of his eyes. There didn't seem to be any rhyme or reason to it. Just like people, some dogs simply didn't care for each other.

Rebel was fond of other Setters and medium-sized, smooth-coated, longhaired dogs, especially females. Being a feisty Celt, he tangled only with ferocious brutes like his mortal enemy, my neighbor's champion Akita that outweighed him by forty pounds. When spoiling for trouble Reb's motto seemed to be "The bigger and badder, the better."

Over the next few weeks we crossed paths with Otto and Bettina so often that it felt like they were stalking us. Our complex isn't large so it was only a matter of time before the dogs would meet up close. I wasn't particularly worried: Otto is more grouchy than aggressive. Even if he snapped and went Mike Tyson on us, I was confident that I could separate them. But what if things jumped off when Eugenie had Tanner? She and Bettina are both rail thin. Muscling two large, powerful dogs would be tough, if not impossible, for them. To forestall that, I decided to let the boys meet on neutral turf when I'd be there to referee.

We were just beginning our walk one morning when I spied Bettina and Otto heading for "Poop Park," an overgrown dirt tract at the end of our complex. We ditched our usual route and hurried to join them. I asked Bettina if she'd mind letting the dogs get acquainted. She looked uneasy but nodded okay. The moment that we dropped the leashes they went nose-to-nose, like Doc Holiday and Johnnie Ringo at the OK Corral. I held my breath. If my experiment went south and Tanner came home bleeding, there'd be hell to pay.

Luckily, they didn't throw down. They stood there for a moment sniffing each other fiercely. Then Tanner broke away and started to spin in circles, inviting Otto to join him in some puppy play. Otto declined. He was too busy gumming the nasty tennis ball clamped in his mouth. It wasn't a love-in but we'd met the neighborhood alpha and lived to tell about it.

When Bettina first got him, Otto was all raw energy and instinct, a wild thing to rival Reggie. Now, after months of patient training, he was calm if not exactly mellow. His marked transformation gave us hope that Tanner would eventually turn out okay. In size, athleticism, and energy, he and Tanner were well matched. Sadly, except for the beach which is technically off-limits, there was nowhere for them to play. For years there were rumors that the City planned to build a dog park, and progress did move at a glacial pace, but Tanner and I lived to see it finally open last year.

Maybe he was aping Otto, or maybe it was Tanner's way of claiming victory but, when he stopped to relieve himself, he lifted his leg for the first time. That same afternoon he found his Big Dog bark. Until then, he'd uttered just two tiny, muted "woofs," his anxious commentary on the new surroundings. Eugenie and I were upstairs reading when a young neighbor started to shout on his cell phone in the alley. He was fighting with his girlfriend, his voice so loud and agitated that you'd have sworn he was inside our home. Tanner leaped up and answered with a thunderous basso that shook the walls. Message delivered, he returned to his bed.

Tanner rarely barked, but he was always on guard. Even when sleeping he laid curled up facing the door, alert for any strange sound or movement that might signal danger. Then, one evening while we were watching TV, he rolled over onto his side and exposed his belly. It was an offer that we couldn't refuse. We gently stroked his soft, pink flesh. He tensed for a moment then closed his eyes and drew back his lips in a contented doggie smile. We were smiling too. This was what we'd wanted when we made him part of our family.

~~~

I kept hoping that these small victories would carry over to the car. The morning after his belly rub I took Tanner to the market with me. I left him in the Chrysler while I did the shopping. I was gone maybe thirty minutes and he seemed fine…until we drove through the gate to pick up Eugenie, who was exercising with Roberta in the Colony. As I drove past the guard, Tanner heaved his guts out. I didn't shout or swear, but inside I was churning. That was enough for Tanner, who spent the rest of the day hiding in his bed.

While I could see how my anger unnerved him (hell, it unnerved me), Tanner's auto anxiety had us baffled. Most dogs love to ride in cars. Dudley insisted on joining us whenever we went out. He'd perch on my lap and bounce along to Aerosmith or Springsteen while we ran errands or visited friends. During my six-year penance in the cab, Rebel often kept me company up front. It was a blatant violation of the Taxi Commission rules, yet complaints were rare. Caught up in the hustle and bustle of the city that never sleeps, harried patrons enjoyed the brief brush with nature that my canine co-pilot provided.

Drugs weren't working for Tanner, so perhaps motion sickness wasn't really the problem. Maybe something terrible had happened to make him dread the car, something connected to the long, ugly scars on his stomach and the bite marks on his neck. When he was just a pup, had he been driven to abandoned buildings or vacant lots and forced to test his mettle in the fight ring? Found wanting, was he beaten for his cowardice, then thrown away to survive on the streets as best he could, competing with other strays for scraps and garbage? He couldn't, or wouldn't, say.

Thinking about it made me want to hurt the bastards who'd mistreated him. Eugenie urged me to "see it differently." For her, Tanner's scars were beauty marks. Instead of hating his abusers, she said that we should be grateful to them. Without their unkindness and neglect he'd have never found his way into the shelter, and into our lives.

Understanding Tanner's troubled history didn't help him, or me. It seemed like every day brought another mess, and another angry, knee-jerk reaction. He was trying hard to please us and be a good dog. I knew that. Unfortunately for both of us, his emotional radar was far more sensitive than I'd ever imagined.

I didn't mean to frighten him but I couldn't get myself under control. Sometimes I smoldered for days on end, caught in the throes of a malaise that I could neither name nor dispel. Most of the time, my fury took me unaware like a leg cramp that strikes when you're stretching peacefully in bed. For almost as long as I could remember I had had these "seizures": visceral, overwhelming, burning "itches" that had to be scratched. Every explosion left me more dejected, more hopeless, and more likely to fly off again.

They say that it takes twenty-one days to make or break a minor habit, and much longer for deep-rooted ones. I'd spent a lifetime refining anger into an art form. Continually fuming and chafing, I'd rubbed myself so raw that the slightest disturbance sent me over the edge. I desperately wanted to help Tanner vanquish his demons and lead a happy life. To do that, I'd first have to overcome my own. So far, the prospects weren't good.

~~~

Once he was finally getting full rations, Tanner took to doing his *business* in the bushes by the communal koi pond. I tried to dissuade him but he was adamant; this shady nook was *his* spot. We always scoop (just try leaving dog droppings on a New York sidewalk!), but tempers were running high around our complex, where residents were divided over a contentious move to recall the Board of Directors. The last thing that we wanted was our neighbors hassling us about Tanner's bathroom habits.

Dog people know that it's a guaranteed slam-dunk that your pooch will always "go" at the worst possible time and place. You might spend hours strolling the beach or hiking mountain trails but Bowser will hold it until he's back on the block, squatting on the manicured lawn of that persnickety cat lady next door.

Rebel was particularly tough in that regard. Fearful of soiling his long, feathery coat, he would zigzag down the City streets like a crazed punt returner, dropping bomb-lets in front of repulsed throngs. With Reb, one baggie would never do. I always left the apartment armed with several sections of *The New York Times*. For us, their hallowed motto should have been, "All The News, And Fit For Sh-t."

Reb's crowning moment came during a vacation on Cape Cod. Desperate to escape the urban hubbub, we had scrimped and saved for a two-week getaway, our version of the Fresh Air Fund. We'd just arrived. After we settled into our cottage, I took him for a run at a State Beach in North Wellfleet. I unclipped his collar and off he sped over the dunes. I huffed after him. Sucking wind, I crested an imposing sand hill to find him hunched over, grinning wickedly, doing what comes naturally in front of a scowling Park Ranger. I apologized profusely, blaming the bracing sea air and Reb's city bowels.

~~~

It had been nearly a month, and Tanner was still skittish around people including us. If we dropped a pen or slammed a door he would bolt like we'd fired off an Uzi. Dogs, however, were another matter. Regardless of breed, age, or sex, he was determined to befriend them all. With his massive head and rippling muscles, he cuts an imposing figure. His fellow canines didn't care but Tanner's physique gave their human parents pause, especially when he was charged up (which was all the time) and their pets were small, like my neighbor's Shih Tzu, Ceba.

Watching Tanner drag me across the road, Doug was wary of greeting the new stud. Ceba wasn't. He held his ground and sniffed Tanner from stem-to-stern. Having made his point, he hoisted his tail and led us down the sidewalk, pimp-rolling like a 4-legged gangsta with his posse in tow. Whenever Ceba stopped to mark the bushes, Tanner followed suit. It was their version of social networking, where dogs friend each other by peeing on walls instead of writing on them.

~~~

Much like St. Paddy's Day in Boston, Cinco de Mayo is a full-blown if unofficial holiday in Southern California. In the spirit of the fiesta we took Tanner with us to our local café for enchiladas. While we waited for our order, I jokingly called him *perito* (little dog), trilling the *r* the way I was taught by my *profesoras*. He tilted his head and stared at me like he recalled the epithet, or at least the sound. Were his first owners Latino? He was found wandering in Oxnard, which has a large Latino community, but we'll never know for sure unless he learns to speak or write.

At the restaurant, Tanner drew a gaggle of female admirers including the hostess of a cable TV animal show. From the bite marks on his muzzle she guessed that he had been a *bait dog*, a passive animal used to rile up more promising canine fighters. It fit with our theory. It was painful to imagine him being mistreated but, if he hadn't been, who knows where he might have ended up? Certainly not with us. Change one rock in a stream, or one episode in a life, and you alter its entire course.

After lunch we coaxed Tanner into the car and drove to the beach. As we neared the ocean, he sat up and poked his snout out the window, inhaling the salt air. We parked the car and hit the sand. Or, rather, I hit the sand. Tanner hung back like a newbie at a Tony Robbins fire walk.

I forged ahead and he reluctantly fell in behind me...until we reached the water's edge. Eyeing the endless blue expanse, he dug in his heels and stared at me, wide-eyed. If I was dumb enough to go there, fine. But I was going without him! We saw no point in risking another phobia, so we retreated to the safety of the dunes. Tanner was relieved. He pranced on ahead of us, tossing back his head, savoring the myriad smells of this awesome new place. He was so distracted that he even forgot about the camera, which allowed us to take some pictures with him, our first "family" photos.

As we headed back to the car, a pack of Harleys thundered by. Tanner freaked and broke into a full gallop. Eugenie went flying, soaring for a brief moment like a skinny human kite. Then she thudded back to earth and was towed through the dunes like a klutzy water skier who'd run aground.

Tanner was sandy from the beach and in need of a bath. Neither of us wanted to wrestle him into the tub, or risk having him dive through the shower door, so we hosed him down in the alley behind our place. He winced and struggled to break free as chilly water stung his delicate pink skin. By the time we finished, I was drenched, too.

While we were toweling off a neighbor came by to tell us that one of his dogs, a puppy, had disappeared while they were hiking a local trail. My first reaction was to rip him for needlessly putting the dog in harm's way by letting him run free in an unsafe place like the park, which abuts the Coast Highway and where there's no shortage of predators. Instead, I caught myself and tried to see it differently. I realized that I wasn't really angry; I was upset by the pup's demise and sorry for the owner's loss. I was also frightened by the possibility, however remote, that a similar tragedy could befall Tanner.

Yes, I was scared and had been nearly all my life. Admitting it was a big step. Like most men I'd been trained to ignore fear as a weak and cowardly emotion. Watching my father storm and bluster, I'd learned that being tough and aggressive was preferable to feeling vulnerable. That fight, not flight, was the answer.

My mother played her part, too.

A child of the Great Depression whose fireman father died in the line of duty, she left home at fourteen when her mother's new husband grew "interested" in her and her younger sister. Armed with only a grade school education, she talked her way into a waitress gig at New York's then-swanky Hotel Pennsylvania. She used her meager wages to support them both, making "poor man's eggs" (an egg stretched with corn starch and flavored with bacon grease, served with stale bread) for breakfast, lunch, and dinner.

When she married my father, she thought that she'd found her fairy tale ending. For a short time they were deliriously happy. Then came four kids, the gambling, and the girlfriends; things turned poisonous.

She lived with the "enemy", his immigrant parents who blamed her for his failings. Since her siblings were either struggling or dead, leaving was out of the question. The passionate, caring woman who taught me to play baseball and love books (no *Winnie the Pooh* in our house; I cut my teeth on *Kidnapped* and *Perry Mason*) learned to match my father's bullying in volume if not vehemence.

Everyone needs a shoulder to cry on. She turned to me, her oldest, and poured her heart out, detailing my father's myriad transgressions, her tragic childhood, and her missed opportunities. Her sorrow was palpable, and I was helpless to fix it. It left me sad, frustrated, and angry, totally convinced that there was no justice in the world. No wonder I was having a hard time controlling my temper.

Tanner was a perfect symbol of my predicament. Pit Bulls are often seen as mean, angry dogs, and he looked pretty menacing. Underneath that fearsome appearance, however, was a timid, gentle soul. Like him, I seemed to be tough when I was really frightened: frightened that I couldn't change, that my anger would get the best me as it always had, that I would fail my dog, my wife, and myself. Tanner could feel my fear and it only worsened his, the very thing that we didn't want. Thankfully, unlike me, he wasn't acting out. Yet. If I kept on storming or raging at the world, maybe he'd follow my example. Then what would we do?

Wet and annoyed, Tanner retreated to his bed until it was time for Course In Miracles. With its fertile orchards, luxurious gardens, and majestic shade trees, The Farm is a magical place. Tanner enjoyed it, too, especially the lush lawn that he devoured like a starving goat. When dogs eat grass they usually vomit. Not Tanner. We had the car for that.

We must've inspired Carl and Roberta, because they brought Charlie to class. While we humans worked to still our restless minds, Tanner played the clown. Tail beating a giddy rhythm on the bamboo floor, he rolled onto his back, beckoning his little buddy to romp with him. "Om Shanti Om!" We tried to focus, but they were too cute to ignore. Finally Carl put Charlie on his lap, Tanner settled down, and we got on with the lesson, which dealt with responsibility as a key to love and forgiveness in personal relationships. I was learning that that was crucial with rescue dogs, too.

As Ed explained it, choosing to see things differently allows us to stop viewing ourselves as victims—of the world, other people, our past mistakes—and to accept responsibility for creating the feelings we experience, along with the sad, anxious, angry lives that we fashion from those choices.

When we suffer a loss or disappointment – a romantic breakup, an economic downturn, a career reversal – we can choose to see it as happening 'to' us or 'for' us. In the first case, we're victims of the external world and its uncontrollable forces. In the latter, we're students, eagerly embracing the Life lessons we need to learn to grow and flourish. Change your perception; change your reality. In theory, it sounds simple, like telling a novice karate student to relax when sparring. In practice, it was brutally hard, but not impossible. I'd done it with my neighbor. The question was, could I continue and build upon it?

## Tanner's Friends

*Otto*

*Tanner & Dexter*

## **Tanner's Friends**

*Ceba*

*Dudley*

## Tanner's Friends

*Tanner and Lola*

*Tanner & Taco*

# CHAPTER 6
# JUNE GLOOM

St. Mary's gym is jammed with screaming kids and frantic parents; the grammar school title is at stake. It's nip and tuck as the game winds down. Half a head taller than my teammates, I crash the boards, sending normal-sized boys bouncing like bowling pins. The blubbery, timid kid with glasses, he's now Godzilla sacking Tokyo. The ref blows his whistle. Two free throws, no time on the clock. Sink one for a tie, two for a trophy. Waiting for the ball, I search the bleachers. She's there, of course. My mother. Right up front like always. But where is he? Where is my father?

Later, my teammates and I celebrate at the restaurant with Cokes and pizza. He crows to the staff that his son hit the big shot, won the game, the game he didn't see. Screw that. Screw him.

~~~

*Tanner on Malibu Colony Beach*

In Italian, *mammone* means "mama's boy," a grown man so attached to his mother's apron strings that he sits around sipping espresso and watching soccer while she slaves away tending to his every need. My mother toiled but she was German, not Italian. She insisted that my brother and I do our share of the chores. We grumbled about it then, but those domestic skills have served me in good stead.

In our deal, Eugenie cooks while I do the dishes and heavy cleaning. Since Tanner's arrival, though, I'd been slacking off. The rugs had layers of dog hair. The floors were covered with paw prints. The kitchen and bathroom were so grimy that they needed sandblasting. It took me the better part of a day but, by evening, the place was sparkling. The only thing left was Tanner's crate. I wriggled inside and started to sweep up crumbs, the evidence of our bedtime bribes. As I smoothed the blankets, something slammed into me from behind! It was Tanner, jabbing me with his snout, warning me to quit his crib and stop messing with his stuff. Too bad I didn't take the hint.

That night we replaced his ratty old mattress with a new, velour bed that was filled with aromatic cedar shavings. We were sure that he'd love it. When we swapped them out, he suffered a full-scale meltdown. He began to pace nervously back and forth, darting in and out of the crate, frantically trying to collect his stash of toys before we stole them, too. The fancy bed was too big for the kennel, so we were forced to switch them back. By then, though, the damage was done. When we put him to bed that evening, Tanner was still distraught and panting hard.

Come morning we found him whining and shivering like when he first arrived. His stuffed Dachshund, "Bluie," was soaked with drool. He'd spent a tortured night mouthing his "baby" for comfort, the way a child might clutch a tattered old blanket. We felt guilty and longed to coddle him. We resisted; giving him attention would only reinforce his negative reaction. Like me with my anger, his panic attacks were something that he'd have to work through on his own. Hopefully he would be smarter, and quicker, than me.

The following evening Tanner refused to even approach the crate. After some fruitless pleading I banished Eugenie and muscled him inside. The struggle left us both winded. I felt rotten, and conflicted. It was obvious Tanner would be happier in our room. But he snores, and Eugenie is a very light sleeper, so there was nothing to do but suck it up and live with the status quo.

~~~

Mother's Day was Tanner's "coming out" party. Shortly after noon, Eugenie's family arrived en masse: her mom, Melissa, her dad, Gene, step-mom, Sandra, sister, Stephanie, Steph's husband Ernie, and their teenage son, Armand. They all went gaga for Tanner, especially Ernie who said that he reminded him of Maynard, his miniature Bull Terrier.

Like Tanner, Mayne-dog was sweet, obedient, and low key. Except with his toys. Whenever we visited, Maynard and I used to play fetch in the hallway of their condo. He'd always retrieve the ball, but he hated to "give." When I tried to pry it loose, he'd clamp down, and I'd end up hoisting thirty pounds of wriggling muscle into the air where he'd hang, suspended, until my arm turned to jelly.

After the relatives cleared out, Bonnie, Wren, and Winnie dropped by for a visit. While we were chatting outdoors, Tanner was calm and demure. Then we invited them inside for a cup of tea. Tanner morphed into a dervish. Ears pulled back in a broad grin, he careened around the living room, wriggling, jumping, and spinning in circles, daring Winnie to join him. Bedtime traumas forgotten, he was the happiest dog in the world. At least for the moment.

When we turned down the covers that night, Eugenie found a surprise tucked beneath her pillow: a photo keychain of a tan and white Pit Bull puppy that looked exactly like Tanner. He wouldn't reveal how he managed to buy and smuggle in the gift, but he did say that he was thrilled to have such a sweet, devoted mom.

~~~

After four weeks, Tanner's threshold for car rides had reached all of ten minutes. Even then there was no guarantee that the vehicle would stay dry. Any longer trip, though, boosted the odds that we'd need to clean up after him. I suggested that we leave him behind when we went out, but Eugenie wouldn't have it. She was adamant that we be with him as much as possible in order to speed his adjustment. Restaurants, movies, dancing—we turned down any engagement that didn't include Tanner. Our social calendar was nearly blank. If we didn't start to push the envelope, we'd run the risk of becoming "dog people," those canine-obsessed recluses who never go anywhere without their four-legged children.

When friends invited the three of us to dinner, we jumped at the chance. If we drove slowly, and I stayed calm, we figured that Tanner might survive the twenty-minute drive to neighboring Pacific Palisades. Traffic was snarled that night, and it took that long just to reach the Malibu Pier. Tanner was already queasy, (if the car were a boat, his drooling would have swamped us), but we made it to our friends' house with no spillage.

We spent a pleasant evening with Toni, Ron, and their poodle, Leo. They had rescued him several months before we began to look for a dog. It was their example, in fact, that helped convince us to take the plunge with Reggie. Despite that, we still liked them. We thought for sure that Tanner and Leo would hit it off—after all, they were both shelter dogs—but Leo wasn't in the mood for company. He answered Tanner's playful entreaties with bared fangs and hostile growls.

By the time we finished the last of the wine and set off for home, traffic had eased. Instead of lying prone and slavering, his SOP, Tanner ventured across the back seat to my side of the car. Balancing on my lap, he stuck his head out the window and huffed in the night air. We were heartened by his show of courage. Perhaps our luck had changed and he was finally headed in the right direction.

His predecessor, Reggie, wasn't scared of the car. Just the opposite. He rode facing backwards, peering out the rear window. Whenever he spotted a bird, and there are lots of birds in Malibu, he'd dash back and forth from one side of the car to the other, howling like a banshee. Whenever I tried to restrain him, I felt like the late Steve Irwin wrestling a monster crocodile.

Although Reggie had been gone only a short time, the traces of his stay were already fading. That night, as Tanner and I set off on our walk, I grabbed a baggie from the chest by the door. Inside, I found some silly animal crackers that Reggie's original owners had sent along with him. After Tanner did his business, I forked them over, happy for both dogs and the way things had worked out.

With the clarity of hindsight, our brief, sad stint with Reggie was probably a trial run to help us get our feet wet after so much time without a dog. There was an element of fate about it, too. If we hadn't fostered him, he'd have never found his way to the lady vet who eventually adopted him. And we would never have gotten Tanner.

~~~

In late May I went back to the Agoura shelter to meet with Rob Lerner, a volunteer and licensed animal behaviorist. I'd been flirting with the idea of working with dogs, or at least writing about them, and Rob graciously let me tag along while he exercised some of the "residents," including Joey, an imposing gray Pit that had been brought in several weeks before Tanner. Rob had spent months trying to rehabilitate Joey for possible adoption. It was a daunting effort. Big, very active, and easily triggered, Joey wasn't a good fit for first-time owners, or someone with children or other pets. On top of that, he had a nervous stomach and suffered from constant diarrhea.

In L.A. County, the dominant breeds like Pit Bulls and Rottweilers have to pass a stringent behavioral test before they're deemed adoptable. The dogs must allow volunteers to take away their food, they must tolerate hard petting of the sort dished out by young kids, and they must be able to approach other dogs without showing aggression. With Tanner, we took the extra step of walking (dragging?) him through the building where they house the cats and rabbits. Our cowardly lion kept his eyes downcast the entire time.

Dogs that fail the test are deemed "not adoptable" and marked for destruction. The lucky ones end up at permanent rescues where animal lovers will accept them, flaws and all. Sadly, that's the exception, not the rule. Rob finally found a home for Joey the day before he was to be put to sleep. Three other Pits, including Nadia who was brought in with Tanner, weren't so lucky. They were euthanized after being judged too risky for adoption. Rob remembered Tanner and thanked us for giving him a loving home.

It's Eugenie and I who were grateful to him and the other volunteers for sparing Tanner a sad, dark fate.

When I got home I found him curled up, dozing in his bed. As I stood watching his massive chest rise and fall, I wondered whether he'd recognize the scents of his former home that I carried with me. If so, I hoped that they wouldn't dredge up memories of a painful past.

~~~

To celebrate the start of summer we went for a run on the Colony beach. It was Tanner's first time off-leash, and he blazed along the shoreline, kicking up showers of sand, taking care that his white-tipped paws never touched water. He wasn't exercising to lose weight or get into shape; he was running for the pure joy of it, because it felt good to open up and let loose. It looked like he'd keep going all the way to San Francisco, but then a graceful young Doberman named Xena happened by. Suddenly my Olympic gold medalist was Casanova. He was so entranced by the Amazon that he lost his bearings and wandered into the ocean where a huge wave wiped him out like a rookie surfer.

Tanner's unbridled exuberance reminded us of Rebel on the day that we let him loose in Central Park. We were living on the Upper East Side and had gone to catch a concert near the Metropolitan Museum. Except for a fenced-in ball field in the Village, Reb had never run free in the City before. He really needed to stretch his legs, so we rolled the dice and set him free. He took off like a rocket, headed due north, and kept going until he disappeared from sight. I was crushed; I'd saved him from the pound and here the ingrate repaid my kindness by ditching me at the first opportunity.

Eugenie and I stood staring blankly at the spot where Rebel had vanished, berating ourselves for being so dumb and wondering what to do. We opted to wait and pray, hoping that someone would find the dog before he wandered out of the park into the traffic-choked streets. After what seemed like a century, a chestnut-red form materialized on the horizon, headed our way. Reb hadn't abandoned us after all. He'd merely gone for a jog and, as Setters are known to do, gotten carried away with the scenery. Panting like a bellows, he chugged on over to us and got the welcome of his life.

~~~

"June Gloom" followed hot on the heels of Memorial Day in Malibu, bringing with it fog and cool temperatures. Our first year living there, it rained all spring, and the lousy weather lasted well into fall. Like a kid who'd been promised a trip to Disneyland but forced to settle for a T-shirt, I felt gypped. And ill.

Before we quit New York, Eugenie's mom graciously supervised the fix-up on our Malibu rental. Under her decorator's eye, the place was painted top to bottom, the floors and furniture were refinished, and new carpeting installed.

The work took all of February. During that time, it rained so fiercely that she kept the doors and windows shut tight, which allowed the petrochemical fumes to reach critical mass. When we boarded the plane that would take us to the Left Coast, we had no idea that we'd be moving into a toxic time bomb.

Shortly after we arrived, my head began to pound. I was green, listless, and in constant agony. I tried aspirin, massage, and meditation. Nothing could blunt the pain. Either I was dying or I was allergic to California. I agreed to give it one more week; then I was flying back to New York where I'd stay until I recovered. In desperation, Eugenie took me to see a homeopath who diagnosed me with chemical poisoning. I scoffed, but I took the little sugar pills and the headaches went away.

~~~

After several dreary weeks the fog lifted, the beach heated up, and I swapped my Uggs for flip-flops. I was thrilled; even hot yoga isn't hot enough for my Mediterranean blood. Tanner was bummed. Unlike Setters, Pit Bulls were engineered for short bursts of intense exertion, not endurance. Hiking the hills or jogging the sand, he plodded along like we'd just run the Death Valley Marathon. During our mountain jaunts, we would see scores of alligator lizards sunning themselves on rocks and fallen trees. Lizards meant that it was snake season, and we would need to be careful, especially at "Poop Park" where there were plenty of bushes and dark, shady places for rattlers to hide.

~~~

As spring gave way to summer, our bedtime tussles escalated. Like a smart guerilla fighter, Tanner kept changing tactics, hoping to wear us down. First, he balked at sleeping in the crate. Then, he refused to enter the house. Now, like a kid wrangling for more TV time, he stretched out our evening walks, dragging us around the complex, pretending he needed to "go." The message was clear: sleeping in a cramped pen away from his pack sucked. His resourcefulness was impressive, yet we were unmoved. We were stuck in a holding pattern until either he gave up, or we gave in.

To ease our guilt, we bought him new toys and treats, including a fat, juicy shinbone. When we set it on the floor, he nudged it with his snout and backed away. He'd never had a real bone before and hadn't a clue what to do with it. I could relate.

Senior year in high school, our vaunted basketball team played a tournament in Vermont. For blue-collar gym rats that had never set foot outside New Jersey it might as well have been Homer's *Odyssey*. On the bus ride through New England, we stopped at a roadside inn where a harried waitress ran down the lunch menu.

"You get chicken or Salisbury steak," she growled. "Baked potato, butter or sour cream."

She turned to me, seated at the head of the table. I agonized long and hard before ordering the chicken…and the baked potato. Sure, I liked butter and sour cream but, if we could have only one, the potato seemed the obvious choice. My teammates followed suit until our coach stepped in and patiently clarified the situation.

The next morning, Tanner got another crack at his bone. This time, he hunkered down on the bedroom balcony and gnawed away until he'd rooted out the last hint of marrow. Lazing in the sun, snouting the air, he was the picture of nirvana, a far cry from the jittery stray we first brought home.

~~~

Given the likelihood that he was mauled when he was young, Tanner's affection for dogs was nothing short of amazing. He really adores puppies, and he was beside himself when we encountered Trouble, a neighbor's baby Pit Bull. I was late for work and gently tried to nudge him along. Tanner refused to budge. He and the pup spent the next ten minutes tussling on the sidewalk, slapping paws and clacking teeth like rabid wolverines. When I finally managed to pull him away, I hustled him into the car and we drove to the Colony to exercise with Carl.

It was the Fourth of July, and the normally sleepy enclave was jammed with boisterous partygoers. Tanner and Charlie stood guard by the gate while Carl and I got our pump on in the gym. Afterwards, I let Tanner loose to play with some Labs that were chasing driftwood in the surf. The Retrievers inspired him: he insisted on fetching a ratty ball he dug out from the seaweed.

When he grew bored with the ball, he took off to see his Doberman girlfriend who was locked up on the deck. That didn't stop Romeo. Bounding up the stairs, he nuzzled her through the gate, earning us a reprimand from Xena's masters. Not content with trespassing, Tanner leaped down and lit out after a daintily coiffed Bichon, scaring the pants off the owner and her nattily clad guests.

After I rinsed him off, we met Eugenie at the Lumber Yard for some holiday shopping. It was Tanner's first time in a store, and we thought he might panic. He actually enjoyed the shops, especially the salesgirls who "oohed" and "aahed" and showered him with treats. With his big, soulful eyes and sad personal history, if Tanner were human, he'd be a total *playa*.

In the evening, he stayed home while we drove back to Carl's for a cookout supper and front row seats at the annual fireworks. Lounging on the beach as powerful explosions shake the earth and rivers of color rain down on the Pacific is a visceral, magical experience. We left early to be with our dog. We found him quaking in the dark, burrowed into his bed like a tick on a deer, a casualty of the neighborhood kids and their cherry bombs.

It's odd, the things that set dogs off. Like their idiosyncratic human counterparts, some will doze through a hurricane but wig out when the teakettle whistles. While Rebel didn't mind the bustling throngs or the city din, he hated loud arguments. Before our couples' therapy, there were plenty of those, usually about former girlfriends who wanted to "keep in touch."

There's nothing wrong with friendly exes, per se, but I'd failed to establish any kind of boundaries, or to make clear that my relationship with Eugenie was special. Taking their cue from me, the girls treated Eugenie like the housekeeper who was there to forward messages and invitations to events that didn't include her. Eugenie didn't like it, especially when they called in the middle of the night, and she wasn't shy about letting me know. I thought that she was overreacting, trying to control my friendships. Things eventually reached a head, and she gave me a choice: "Get those bitches in line, or I'm gone!"

We were standing by the sofa, screaming at the top of our lungs, when we looked around and noticed Rebel was missing, which was an impressive feat in a 700-square-foot studio. We checked the kitchen alcove and under the bed, but no dog. After several fruitless sweeps, we pulled back the plastic curtain and found him cowering in the bathtub. Whenever things got noisy (I hadn't yet resolved to face my demons), the tub remained his bunker of choice.

Unlike Reb, who was normally even-tempered and unflappable, nearly everything set our Dalmatian, Roxanne, on edge. Instead of cowering, she would whine in a pitch that made your ears bleed. I eventually learned to tune it out. Like Poe's *Tell-Tale Heart*, it drove Eugenie crazy.

One evening, about a year after we had moved to Malibu, she finally snapped. I put the dogs to bed in their kennels but Roxanne was amped and wouldn't quiet down. Convinced that she'd come around, I urged patience and turned out the lights. Half an hour later, I was dead asleep when Eugenie shook me awake.

"Go downstairs and shut her up!" she shrieked.

I tried to reason with her, but she was beyond that. Way, way beyond that. Years of neurotic squealing had pushed her over the edge.

"Make her be quiet…or I'll kill her!"

I pulled on my shorts and trudged down to the garage. I would never hurt the dog, but I had to do something. I started pounding on the kennel and slapping my thighs, cursing like Tony Soprano. I was sure the ruse would fail, that my wife would make good her threat and slaughter me in the bargain. Miraculously, Roxanne grew silent and fell asleep.

~~~

After the July 4th shelling, a tranquil walk was a godsend. Instead of rushing home, Tanner and I lingered on the bench by the koi pond, basking in the morning sun. Glancing through the pine boughs, I caught a glimpse of my neighbor's cat, Sadie, perched on the balcony railing behind us. Squinting like a Delta Force sniper, she had a bead on us, just in case we stepped out of line.

After breakfast, Tanner took a nap to calm his still-jittery nerves while we drove across the hill to buy new carpet for the bedroom and office. Eugenie chose a stylish broadloom (tan, of course) guaranteed to withstand anything that a rambunctious Pit Bull might dish out. Or so we were told.

To install the carpet, we had to move the furniture, so I decided to re-paint my office, too. I was cleaning brushes in the garage when Tanner crept downstairs to check on me. It was his first voluntary foray into the dank lair of the dreaded car. I was so startled to see him that I dropped a gallon of paint, spattering the washer, the car, and myself. Sudden movements and loud noises usually spooked him, but he came charging to inspect the mess. I had to act fast, but what to do? Chase him off and risk another setback in our checkered relationship, or spend days scrubbing paint from the rugs and floors? Hands held aloft like a Jackson Pollock scarecrow, I maneuvered my butt between him and the latex puddle, then boogied him back upstairs like we were dancing on *Soul Train*.

~~~

Gasping for breath between crunches and push-ups, a client once confided to me that his wife and kids were kicking back at a Montana dude ranch while he stayed behind to learn whether or not their five-year-old had been accepted to a private preschool. Vetting young kids was "messed up," he acknowledged, but with 500 applicants and only two-dozen spots, it was a big deal for anxious parents. The admission process is so fierce, he explained, that friends would conceal their choice of schools to lessen the competition.

Eugenie and I agreed that we were lucky we didn't have kids, so we would get to skip that particular madness. Thanks to Tanner, we came to eat our words, sandwiched between two slices of crow, with humble pie for dessert.

On a dare from a friend, I had scheduled an audition for *Who Wants To Be A Millionaire* in New York City, where it's shot. Normally we would have welcomed a chance to visit friends and family, but we were concerned about finding someone to look after Tanner. Kennels are okay for a short stay, provided they are clean, safe, and allow for a happy, playful experience. With the tryout looming, we checked several facilities and found them lacking in one or more of the essentials.

By chance, I mentioned this to Rob Lerner, the behaviorist and shelter volunteer. Rob said that he and his wife, Diane, occasionally boarded dogs at their home. Depending on the dates, they'd consider watching Tanner…providing he first passed a meet-and-greet with Sunny, their yellow Lab. Forget about landing a place in some tony kindergarten; we would have to fight for a spot in doggie day-care! Hypocrites that we are, we jumped at the chance and crafted what we felt was a surefire strategy.

On the day of the big "interview", we gave Tanner plenty of exercise so that he wouldn't be too rough with Sunny. We withheld his dinner so that he wouldn't hurl in the car and show up stinking of vomit. We arrived early and took a long constitutional so that he wouldn't queer the deal by dumping on their lawn. Having covered all the bases, we rang the bell and uttered a silent prayer that Tanner would be on his best behavior.

Boy, was he ever. He was friendly and playful but not overly so. He inspected their well-kept yard but didn't poop or water the shrubs. He responded happily to Rob and his wife, going so far as to lie on his side for them. And he even let the very submissive Sunny push him around a bit. Tanner was cute, smart, and charming...the perfect dog.

We spent an hour extolling his virtues, then we said goodbye and drove off, our fate hanging on the outcome of a "conversation" between the Lerners and their four-legged dean of admissions.

If Tanner made the cut, Diane said that he would get to stay with Sunny in their bedroom. That must have gotten Eugenie thinking because she offered to let Tanner sleep in our room that night. Given her issues—she wears earplugs, uses a sound machine, and has equipped the place with blackout drapes—it was a huge step and a sign of how much she loved the dog.

Like a death row inmate who'd been granted a last-second reprieve, Tanner curled up into a tiny ball, trying hard to make himself invisible in case we changed our minds. Eugenie said that he woke her several times with his snoring. I didn't hear a thing. Then again, I slept right through the 6.7 Northridge Earthquake. I was rooting for the new arrangement. Secretly, I doubted that it would last a week.

Try forty-eight hours.

Early on the third night Eugenie roused me to complain about Tanner's "ear flapping." With a heavy heart, I moved dog and bed into my office. As I shut the door, he eyed me with guilt and confusion. He was being punished and had no idea why.

***Tanner's first bone***

# DOGS & RATTLESNAKES

### Rattlesnake Bites

Most rattlesnake venom is "hemotoxic", meaning that it compromises the integrity of blood vessels, causing swelling that impairs circulation and normal clotting, which can lead to uncontrolled bleeding, shock, and death. The venom of the Mojave rattler is "neurotoxic," causing rapid paralysis of the respiratory system and suffocation.

The seriousness of a bite depends on the type of snake, the size of the dog, and the amount of venom injected. Some bites are "dry" (no venom injected), and only a small percentage of bites are fatal, but all snakebites should be considered serious and treated as emergencies, even in vaccinated dogs. Facial bites are particularly serious, since swelling may block the throat or hinder the ability to breathe. Seek immediate veterinary attention and do not try to cut the bite wound open or suck out the poison.

### Treatment

<u>IV Fluids</u>. Since the most common cause of death from snakebites is circulatory failure, IV support (administration of fluids via catheter), and blood pressure monitoring are very important.

<u>Antivenin</u>. Antivenin can be very helpful in the inactivation of snake venom but there is a narrow window (approx. 4 hrs.) during which it must be used. It's especially crucial with small dogs (and

cats), since the amount of venom they receive per pound is much greater than with large dogs.

Antihistamines. Injected antihistamines may help with the inflammation from the actual bite and in preventing possible anaphylactic reaction to antivenin.

**Prevention**

Vaccination. Rattlesnake vaccine offers protection against the venom of the Western Diamondback and the other rattlers except the Mojave Rattlesnake. Most dogs require two-three doses at a cost of approximately $30/dose. Vaccination offers protection equal to two vials of antivenin, which runs several hundred dollars per vial.

Avoidance Training. Through the use of a shock collar, the trainer applies a mild stimulus to teach the dog to avoid the sound, smell, and sight of defanged or muzzled reptiles. Check to see if your local Parks & Recreation Department offers avoidance training. In Malibu, group classes start at around $70.00.

**Resources**

- Dr. Howie Baker, DVM

# CHAPTER 7
# GOING HOME

*I'm eighteen and just out of school, humping a jackhammer and busting concrete slabs at a copper plant in the dead of summer. In a week's time, we'll drop a man on the moon. In a month, the Woodstock Nation will be born in the mud at Yasgur's farm. Then I'm off to college. Right now, though, all I care about is lunch and a chance to soothe my throbbing arms. The whistle shrieks, and workers race off to the bars for shots and nasty food. I could join them, these "men" with union books, wives and kids, but I'm just slumming and they know it. Instead, I head to the family restaurant and the sweet fennel sausage cooking in the oven. I'll wrap it in just-baked bread and swig a birch beer while I ice my cramping wrists.*

*I crack open the door. The air conditioning swallows me up. The bar is empty? The bar is never empty. I can hear my father in the dining room, ranting at his brothers like they're wayward school boys too thick to get the lesson. The restaurant's trusted accountant, a thieving little prick, has died, but not before swallowing five years' worth of taxes. The Government couldn't* care less. They want their money, a hundred large, or they'll seize the business. That means taking out a mortgage, which they'll all have to sign.

Sal shrugs. No point jousting with my father, not when he's cranked up like this. He scrawls his name on the note and leaves. Frank balks. "How do we know this isn't some scam? That you won't go out and blow the money on horses or craps?" A fair question, given his history, but my father isn't fair, not when he's hot, and right now he's beyond steaming. "Sign the goddamn paper, Frankie!" Normally the compliant one, my uncle shakes his head. My father ducks into the closet and returns with a cigar box; inside's a .32. He loads the gun, snaps the cylinder shut. "Sign the paper," he says softly. Frank digs in; he won't be pushed around. "There will be no mortgage…"

A bomb goes off, and Frankie's on the ground, writhing in agony, blood gushing from the hole in his thigh. "For chrissakes, it's just a flesh wound! Sign the paper and we'll get you patched up." My father offers a pen, Frank scribbles his name and they're out the door to a local doctor, a paesano, who'll write it up as an "accident."

~~~

**The writer at Spirito's Restaurant, Elizabeth, NJ**

Tanner had glimpsed the Promised Land, only to be summarily banished. We feared that he might protest by trashing the office or worse. He didn't. In the morning, he seemed genuinely glad to see us, romping around like before, begging for pets and playing with his toys while we pulled ourselves together and made the bed. With Reggie, we'd been forced to hide everything in reach. Tanner had no interest in Tylenol, earplugs or tissues, just his growing collection of toys, his "babies."

After several anxious days, the Lerners phoned to say that he'd been granted a spot in doggie day-care. Our Gotham getaway was a go. Now all we had to do was book the flight. Redeeming reward miles was like piercing my tongue with a nail gun. The service rep offered only crappy flights with lousy times and multiple stops. An hour of tortured haggling and I was ready to walk to New York. Instead, I opted for a little trickery. I hung up and phoned the airline's regular reservation line. Curiously, the clerk "found" several decent flights that weren't available from the awards people just minutes before. When she requested payment, I acted confused.

"This isn't the Frequent Flyer number?" I asked in my best old geezer voice.

The clerk explained my "mistake" and booked the flight with our miles. Hmm.

Tanner didn't give a fig about my airline hassles; he just wanted me to win big, so we could buy him more toys and a new car. I told him that would never happen unless they invented one that was waterproof, with built-in air freshener.

Actually, things had improved dramatically in that department, largely because we'd given up. Unless it was absolutely necessary, we had been keeping Tanner away from the car. Eugenie felt that we were copping out, forestalling the inevitable. I saw it as a win-win: the dog had stopped puking and I'd quit going ballistic. Only I hadn't, not really. I still fumed over lost keys, missing buttons, snagged zippers, morning traffic, evening traffic, rainy weather, foggy weather, sunny weather, over-cooked pasta, undercooked steak, noisy neighbors, reality TV, and scores of other "life-and-death" matters that made my blood boil. My venom wasn't directed at Tanner, yet it upset him nonetheless. When I could sense a flare-up coming on, I stepped away until the foul mood passed. But usually it came on like a sneeze, and he paid the price.

I was stretched out on the sofa with the sports page one Sunday, Tanner curled up by my feet napping in the sun, just two guys enjoying a lazy morning, when Eugenie popped in to hurry me along.

"You better get moving," she said, her voice tinged with urgency. "We're having brunch in town, remember?"

I didn't. She'd made a date with friends and forgotten to tell me. I'd have to skip the paper, and the workout I had planned.

"Thanks for letting me know!" I bellowed. I leaped up and flung the paper into the kitchen. I didn't see the wine glasses sitting on the counter. Tanner lit out for bedroom. I spent the next half-hour sweeping up shards of my wife's favorite crystal.

~~~

Despite our admissions coup and my airline triumph, Eugenie got cold feet. She stayed home with Tanner while I went off to strike it rich. My connecting flight from Denver was delayed by tornadoes. (Tornados in New York City, but there's no such thing as global warming!) By the time we touched down, I was trashed. My sister, Honey, picked me up, and we drove to our childhood home in Elizabeth, New Jersey. We shared a pizza, and then I crashed out on her sofa.

The following afternoon, Honey schlepped me to the Upper West Side and ABC studios for the qualifying test. Filing inside with the other hopefuls, I felt confident, almost cocky; I'd previously competed on *Jeopardy* and emerged victorious on the syndicated show *Trivial Pursuit*. When I didn't pass, I was stunned. I called

Eugenie with the news. Having come all that way and used up precious frequent flyer miles, I felt that I'd let her down.

"Don't be stupid," she said. "Tanner and I still love you."

I tried to shrug it off, but Honey could sense my dejection. To console me, she suggested we have dinner at Spirito's Restaurant, a landmark eatery that's been in our family for more than eighty years. Unable to scratch out a living in the eastern hills of Campania—"Italy is beautiful," he said, "but you can't eat the view."—my grandfather sailed to America in the early 1900s. Like millions of other desperate immigrants, he tried his hand at various occupations, pharmacist, laborer and gambler among them, before striking pay dirt as a restaurateur.

After a stab at upscale dining, he set up shop in Elizabeth, in the Italian ghetto of Peterstown, aka "The Burg." At the time, industrial firms like Phelps Dodge Copper, Singer Sewing Machine, and the Esso (now Exxon/Mobil) refinery were booming, and their blue-collar workers flocked to the raucous tavern and restaurant for hearty, affordable Neapolitan fare.

The place had its quirks. There were no reservations, so customers were forced to mill about the dining room or wait outside in the biting winter cold or stifling summer heat until a table opened up. There was no butter for the bread, so patrons had to bring their own. And there was no coffee or dessert to linger over, so table turnover was quick. Waitresses memorized the orders and committed them to paper only when presenting the check. To reach the restrooms located in the bar, diners had to venture through the kitchen, a minefield of manic activity, foul language, and hair-trigger tempers.

The regulars included bookies, shylocks, and other assorted hustlers named "Duke", "Shady," and "Jack Rabbit." To call them colorful would be to dub Brando some actor. My father ran the kitchen while his brothers, Sal and Frankie, supervised the bar and food prep. They loved each other but fought like hyenas, even in front of the patrons. I used to tease my dad that the customers came in spite of the staff, not because of them.

And come they did. The place was open seven days a week and packed every night, with the kitchen pushing out 700-plus dinners on Sundays. It was "cash only," and the books were a marvel of accounting creativity. At the height of the dinner madness, Spirito's was *Cheers* meets *Saving Private Ryan* as envisioned by Martin Scorsese.

Despite my setback, I was hungry and looking forward to veal parmigiana and the giant homemade ravioli. For most of my life, the restaurant had been the hub of my family's universe, yet it seemed smaller and less vivid than I remembered, diminished by the passage of time. I hadn't set foot there since my dad's death twenty-five years prior. With him gone, there seemed no point.

Sitting in a wooden booth that he fashioned when he was still a carpenter, before he joined his father and married my mother, random images from my childhood came rushing back: My grandfather holding court in the smoke-filled bar, playing cards with his friends, chewing De Nobili cigars, the foul-smelling "Italian ropes"...My uncles Frank and Sal fighting with customers, then dashing to the betting parlor, a vintage '40s phone booth, to take the locals' "action"…My father pacing behind the stove, a caged jungle cat, his veiny, short-sleeved, burn-scarred arms pounding the bell, demanding the waitresses move their asses and get the orders out…My brother and I as young boys, rumbling around the storeroom, lugging wheels of pungent provolone, stacking cases of tomatoes, olives, pepperoncini, hoping he would notice and tell us that he was impressed, that we're strong, and smart, and good.

A full belly softened the agony of defeat. I called Eugenie and told her I'd decided to give it another shot. I'd go back to ABC the following day for the stand-by auditions. If I passed the test and subsequent interview, I'd have just enough time to make my return flight. Honey could always hit the flashers on her police car and clear the way, providing we made it through the Holland Tunnel into New Jersey.

The next morning, I was first in line. When the test ended, I was called to stay behind. After a warp-speed interview, I joined the survivors waiting to be taped. It was lunchtime on Friday, and things were moving painfully slow. By the time I finished telling a bored cameraman my earnest reasons for wanting to do the show (like, uh, the money, the money and, oh yeah, the money!), it was nearly 1:00. My flight was leaving at 2:15.

Honey met me at the curb with the engine running. We blasted down the Westside Highway, inched our way through the Tunnel, and roared the five miles to Newark Airport. I settled into my seat as they were closing the airplane doors. I felt lucky and invincible, until we landed in Chicago for a brief stopover.

An equipment malfunction (pilot hangover?) meant that I would miss my connection and be forced to spend the night in Chi town. I called Eugenie to let her know. She was upset and said that Tanner would be, too, and that I'd better work some magic. I sprinted to customer service, where I told the rep about *Millionaire,* and how I needed to get home to my despondent rescue dog. She wished me good luck and handed me a boarding pass for the day's last flight to L.A., with an upgrade to boot.

It was after midnight when I landed. Eugenie met me at the gate. We shared a steamy kiss (or five) and then drove home. I'd imagined a delirious welcome from Tanner. He would jump, and wiggle, and lick my face. All I got was a few half-hearted shakes of the tail. Was he sleepy, or miffed that his brief stint as alpha dog was over?

For the next few days, he seemed out of sorts, as if he'd gotten used to a different, gentler rhythm in my absence. His attitude wasn't the only thing that had changed. While we were out walking, we met our neighbor who delivered some disturbing yet predictable news. On the previous evening he had taken his small terriers for an off-leash stroll on the nearby hillside. His three dogs had wandered into the darkness. When he whistled them back, only two returned. And this was barely one month after his pup disappeared on the park trail.

Losing pets is a reality in Malibu. Cats and small dogs regularly fall victim to coyotes, hawks, and owls. This, however, was beyond the pale.

"You're running a god damn drive-thru!" I felt like screaming. "Why not just slather them with catsup and tie them to a tree!"

Instead, I swallowed hard and offered my sympathy. To find true peace, *The Course* says, we must give up judgment. Like my neighbor, I hadn't learned my lesson yet.

When we set out on our walk that night, Tanner kept snouting the air and refusing to heel. The fur on his back was bristled up. At the end of the street, he wheeled around suddenly and bolted for the hillside, where a large coyote stood gazing down at us. The predator that had dispatched my neighbor's dog was cruising for another happy meal.

Tanner was so worked up I had to grab the leash to keep Eugenie from being dragged off her feet. He reared up on his hind legs and roared a full-on challenge: "Whoever you are, whatever you are, if you come for me or my people you'd better come hard, because one of us won't be going home!" The brazen coyote wisely trotted off. Snacking on lapdogs and house cats is one thing; tackling a crazed Pit Bull and two people is another.

Like his feral counterpart, Tanner's behavior was instinctual and honest, devoid of judgment. He bore no animosity toward the coyote; he was merely following the call of his ancestral DNA. Unlike them, I was in a state of perpetual war, seeing threats in everyone and everything. How many times had I snapped over some perceived injustice or injury—a driver cutting me off in traffic, my wife asking me to rearrange the furniture, or a neighbor letting his dogs run free?

According to *The Course*, anger always stems from fear. To get a handle on it, we must first drop our defenses and dispassionately examine the situations that set us off. If we can do that, and it's a pretty big *if*, we'll find that we're "…never upset for the reasons we think."

My dad used anger to distance himself from his wife and children. It enabled him to continue his gambling and philandering, and to avoid confronting his fear that domestic life would squelch his spirit. In the same way, when Eugenie and I started growing close, I'd used anger to stifle our emotional intimacy so that I wouldn't have to face my fear of commitment.

I still practice karate, but I've scaled back my workouts to adjust for my age and the wear and tear on my body. For many years, however, I trained nearly every day, sometimes as much a twenty hours a week.

"You're over-doing," Eugenie would complain. "Normal people don't exercise like that."

I saw her comments as an attack. A bossy shrew, she was criticizing my priorities, meddling with something that was none of her business. Who the hell was she to say what's "normal"? Naturally, I refused to cut back, since doing so would mean that she'd won, and I'd surrendered control of my entire life!

My view was absurd. I should have been flattered, not angry, but I was too emotionally triggered to see it any other way. If I had been able to step back and calmly examine the situation, I might have seen that Eugenie wasn't trying to dictate my life or fence me in. She loved me and missed me when I was off training. For her, karate threatened our budding relationship. Had I chosen to see it differently, instead of escalating our conflict, I might've assured her that there was time and energy enough for her and the dojo. Instead of raised voices and hurt feelings, we'd have been at peace.

Regardless of the circumstances, by living mindfully, not reactively, it's possible to uncover what is really bugging us, and to choose different, more loving responses. I understood the concept. Given my long, abysmal history of unconscious rage and hair-trigger reactions, Tanner was more likely to embrace the coyote.

**The writer & Tanner enjoying some quiet time**

# CHAPTER 8
# TOO SCARY TO LIVE WITH

It's August and the City's a ghost town, the streets hotter than a pizza oven as a million cabbies race frantically, burning fuel, hoping for a miracle or, at least, to make our nut. I stop for a light on lower Park Avenue. A woman opens the door. She's young, hard. "Will YOU take me to Brooklyn?" It's an indictment, not a question.

The money's in Manhattan, not in the boroughs, shuttling white hipsters to restaurants, bars, and clubs. I'm tired, desperate, and more than a little guilty, and so I nod "okay." She whistles and he comes sprinting over. Boyfriend? Husband? Earring, shaved head, muscle shirt, the guy's a dead ringer for middleweight champ Marvin Hagler.

From the jump, they bust my ass, hassling me about the radio, scoffing at the "no smoking" sign. I could kick myself; "No good deed…" We creep through Brownsville into East New York, the end of the earth and dangerous. Where the hell are we going? They fudge directions. The hairs on my neck spring to attention. If

*I'm lucky, they'll take just the money. I slip the blackjack from my bag, and set it on the seat where they can't see.*

*It's near dark when we stop at the projects. She heads off while he stands looking after her, digging in his pockets for the fare. Once she's inside, he tosses crumpled bills through the window—two bucks—and he's off, flying through the courtyard. I abandon the car and tear after him, the blackjack in my hand, a sprinter's baton. He's fast but I'm faster, fueled by fear and outrage. He blasts through the door into the lobby where she's waiting, fumbling with the key. I spin him around, swinging leather-covered lead. He crumples, bleeding. She cringes but I'm past that now and I whack her, too—"Yeah, I'll take you to Brooklyn!"*

*I haul ass to the cab, sitting where I left it, the door agape, engine running. Neighbors mill about, asking what's the fuss. "They robbed me!" I scream, and I'm gone. Heart pumping faster than the Ford's V-8, I race back to the Village, and Eugenie, who asks sweetly, "How was your night?"*

~~~

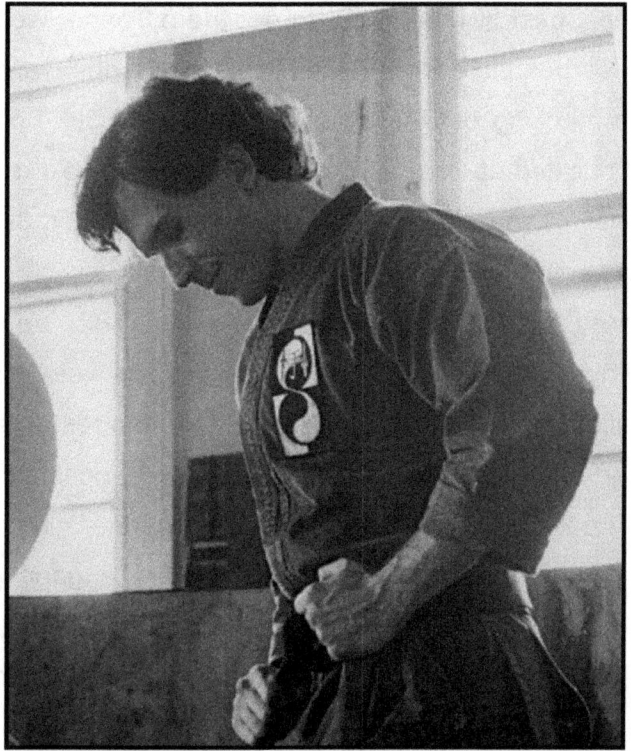
*The writer receiving his black belt, NYC 1988*

Flying cross-country and bunking on my sister's sofa put my back in knots. Fighting to keep Tanner from attacking the coyote finished me off. My muscles were in full spasm, which meant a visit to the chiropractor. So far, we'd been socializing close to home or leaving Tanner behind whenever we ventured out of Malibu. If we wanted a dog that could travel with us, that would eventually have to change. An hour's drive away, Ventura (formally *La Mission de San Buenaventura*) seemed like a good test.

Like new parents wrangling over nap times, we anguished over which route to take. The freeway is shorter than the winding, picturesque Coast Highway, but to get there Tanner would have to brave the serpentine canyon. Either way, the odds were good that I'd end up mucking out the car. We opted for PCH. For emotional support, I buckled up beside him in back. Before we'd even cleared the driveway, Tanner started slobbering like Homer Simpson. He drooled the entire way.

Founded by Father Junipero Serra in 1782, Ventura is an unpretentious mix of surfers, bikers, homeless vets, and middle-class families. It boasts quaint shops, affordable restaurants, and a charming harbor. The chiropractor's office is located behind the Ventura Theater, a venue for live rock concerts. During Eugenie's session, Tanner and I waited outside where a gang of hulking, inked-up roadies was crashing about, unloading amps and gear. Despite the fearsome racket, Tanner bravely stood his ground. Two months ago, he'd have run for the hills and dragged me with him.

After our pummeling, we had lunch at Tony's, a funky little joint where they coax amazing pizza from a battered, century-old oven that's held together with baling wire. Eugenie and I had been spoiled, living in Greenwich Village where we could walk to John's, Arturo's, and Lombardi's. Since moving west, our quest for great pizza had been largely fruitless. Time and again, friends steered us to their favorites only to have us come away under-whelmed. Tony's isn't John's but it's darn good, and a heck of a lot closer.

It's also dog friendly. When we pulled in, a posse of young boarders was camped out on the back patio with a puppy and an older, strapping Pit Bull. Tanner desperately wanted to meet the dogs. We hung back. The big boy seemed friendly but what if he took Tanner's presence as a challenge? We felt like hypocrites. We didn't want people unfairly judging Tanner, and yet here we were doing that very thing with another dog.

When we finished stuffing ourselves, we stopped by the stone yard for sculpture bases. Then we drove back down the coast. Tanner was so drained from all the excitement that he slept the entire way. For a change, I got to ride up front with Eugenie like a normal couple.

Usually, when we arrive home, Tanner bolts upstairs. This time, he hung around the garage while we unloaded the car. He seemed pleased that he'd survived his first road trip without incident. His bright eyes and perky tail spoke volumes: "I'm your dog, and today I did good."

That night, Eugenie sprung him from the office and let him back in our room. He was thrilled, and spent the night curled up in his bed next to mine. Sometime before daylight, he whimpered softly, caught in the throes of a doggie nightmare. I reached down and stroked his flank until he grew still, then I drifted back to sleep.

~~~

*The dream is torturous and always the same, a vivid, primal out-picturing of my powerful, buried conviction that Life's a struggle to the death. I'm covered to the elbows in gore, his precious crimson spattered across my face, flailing, kicking, gouging, fighting for my very life. Still he keeps coming, my nameless, relentless enemy. Who would have thought the bastard had so much blood in him? I seize him by the throat with veiny fingers and squeeze for all I'm worth until something snaps, and I'm jolted awake. I lie there, drawing in painful, ragged breaths, heart racing, arms and legs knotted from the nightly struggle until dawn sets me free.*

~~~

Now that she had the bases, my wife drafted me to mount her newest sculptures. Carving is an exacting, tiring process, and she labors over each piece like a mother giving birth. Stone is hard but also unpredictable. It will sometimes shatter at the slightest touch. Mounting stone sculpture is like dismantling explosives: a bit too much pressure on the drill and months of work—and my domestic bliss—are turned to rubble.

If that weren't pressure enough, I had Eugenie hovering over me, shouting directions, and cursing under her breath. For a change, she was the lunatic. By the time I finished, my hands were trembling and my head was throbbing. In the process, I'd bored a nice, neat hole in my thumb. Eugenie checked to make sure that I hadn't marred the art. Then she thanked me and patched me up. I needed a drink. Or two. Instead of banging down mojitos, I hit the pool.

I'm a lousy swimmer. My physiognomy doesn't help. My body fat is in the single digits, my feet splay out, and my kick's so bad that I move backwards in the water, which is nearly impossible to do. Several years ago, Carl tried to teach me to swim correctly. A lifelong surfer and former high school swim champ, he's a dolphin in the pool. Watching my New York "splash and thrash" was as painful for him as it was for me.

During our initial, and only, session, I arched my back and kept my head aloft, refusing to let it touch the water. If, by chance, my face brushed the surface, I held my breath. By the time he gave up and cut me loose, my neck muscles were so strained that I couldn't swallow solid food for days.

Drilling the bases was torture. Now that we had Tanner bouncing around the house, just living with Eugenie's sculptures was stressful. Our friend and neighbor, Zari, was taking carving lessons from my wife. Sometimes she'd bring along her Wheaton Terrier, Dexter, and tie him to our fence until they'd finished pounding, grinding, and sanding. Dexter didn't mind; he was content just relaxing in the sun. For Tanner, though, being separated from his friend was sheer torture.

I felt bad hearing him moan and whine while the girls were busy busting rocks one day, so I let Dexter inside to play with Tanner. Everything was fine until Dex got tired and sought refuge on the sofa with Tanner's stuffed python, "Snakie," clenched in his teeth. Tanner was indignant; if he wasn't allowed up there, neither was Dexter, especially not with one of his babies.

Tanner seized the snake. One shake of his massive head and Dexter was back down on the floor. A frantic tug of war ensued. As the melee spiraled out of control, they smashed into the coffee table, nearly upending a delicate alabaster nude. Watching it teeter back and forth, I thought of my wife, and all those nasty drills and grinders she plays with. I can't swear that she'd have punished the dogs, but I know for sure that I'd have gotten an ass whipping. I hurriedly secured the art and rushed the boys outside to chill.

~~~

We'd sworn not to bore people with Tanner stories, yet everywhere we went, all we talked about was rescue dogs, Pit Bulls, and Tanner. No place was safe; not parties, not openings, not even bat mitzvahs.

I met Sensei Mel Pralgo shortly after we moved from NYC. We had our roots in the same karate system, and we hit it off immediately. We've been friends ever since. I can remember babysitting his infant daughter at the dojo. She was thirteen now, and celebrating her bat mitzvah, looking glamorous and uncomfortable as girls that age do when thrust into the spotlight.

The party was a blast. In addition to being a decorated karate instructor, Mel is also an accomplished drummer. To get things rolling, he grabbed the microphone and led the guests in a spirited hora, followed by a Limbo contest. It was Simi Valley in 2009, but the vibe was pre-Woodstock Catskills.

I swapped war stories (and tequila shooters) with karate friends, shamelessly exaggerating our past exploits. Strangely, the older we get, the better we were. Former students dropped by to say hello. Like lapsed Catholics, they sheepishly begged absolution—work, family, injuries had kept them away from the dojo—and promised to return to the fold. When I wasn't hearing confession, Eugenie and I tore up the dance floor, dusting off our slickest swing and salsa moves.

We were seated with Mel's son, Rob, who'd flown in from Atlanta. When we mentioned Tanner, his eyes lit up. He whipped out his phone and showed us video of Boomer, a Pit that he'd rescued from a Georgia fight ring. Boomer had been a "training dog," his teeth filed down to keep him from harming more promising combatants. When Rob found him, the dog was in dreadful shape. Besides the emotional scars and dental deformity, he had a full-blown case of heartworm. He weighed just twenty-seven pounds. The vet assumed that Rob had come to put him down, but Rob insisted on trying to save the animal. Boomer was treated and sent home with slim chance for survival. Rob put the dog to bed and fell asleep.

Late that night, he woke to find his new roommate looming over him. Maybe taking in a doggie Rambo who might suffer a sudden, fatal flashback wasn't such a smart move after all. But Boomer didn't snap. The medicine cured the heartworm, the dog gained forty pounds of muscle, and Boomer became a loyal, loved, and totally docile companion.

Rob's video inspired us. We borrowed a friend's Flip and shot some footage of Tanner playing with his toys. The camera spooked him, but we weren't surprised. He was always wary of strange objects, especially phones and small electronic devices. There's an ugly burn mark behind one ear, so it's possible he was zapped with a Taser to punish some transgression or to goad him into fighting.

With his striking looks and sweet disposition, Tanner would be a natural for commercials, if only he wasn't so jumpy. I can see us on the set, beaming proudly, as they holler "Action!" Right on cue, our boy charges for the Alpo. He's about to clean the bowl when a grip knocks over a lighting stand. Tanner freaks and retreats to his dressing kennel. We cajole and plead to no avail; he's too upset to continue. I give the director the bad news; he'll have to shut it down for the day and blow the budget. Furious, he storms off screaming, "You'll never eat bones in this town again!"

~~~

During those first few months, I was on the ropes, treading on eggshells, trying to adapt to the mild-mannered dog that was sharing our home. It wasn't what I'd planned, not even close. Forget about recapturing my youthful zest; I felt old, disgruntled and beset by demons. But Tanner had turned the corner now and was finally settling down. He hadn't vomited in weeks and wasn't flinching nearly as much. I was proud of him. And myself. Despite a rocky start, I'd kept my resolution and gotten my temper in check. Or so I thought.

We were hurrying home from our walk one morning when I found a battered old van blocking our garage. Pepperdine University is just down the road. I figured it was some college kid on an early booty call. Luckily, I'd parked our old Lexus on the street. Eugenie took it to work, while I wrote the offender a matter-of-fact note asking that they please be more considerate. Then I went inside to do the dishes.

I'd barely cleared the table when the bell rang. It was the van owner, a neighbor, and he was hot.

"You have a problem with the way I park, talk to me like a man! Don't leave some chicken-shit note!"

Really? I calmly pointed out that he was the offender, not me.

"Up yours!" he replied.

Three months before, I'd have given him a primer on the creative use of profanity in conversational English, and then booted him out of my house. Instead, I tried using my new spiritual tools. If we're "never upset for the reason we think," why then was he hell bent on ripping me a new one?

Suddenly it hit me—I hadn't sided with his faction in the ongoing HOA dispute.

I'd backed him on numerous other issues, but that didn't matter. I'd refused to join his crusade and for that I was a spineless worm in cahoots with the legions of darkness. Thanks to Eugenie, Tanner, and *The Course*, I'd made headway with my anger, but there was a limit to my patience. As he continued to rant, my Neapolitan blood started boiling like Vesuvius. I grit my teeth and coolly suggested that he'd be doing me, and the entire community a huge favor if he got himself a prescription for Xanax, and filled it.

I was still digesting the screwy encounter when Winnie's "dad," Hiroshi, dropped by to discuss the HOA brouhaha. Was it coincidence, or had the garage blocker recruited him to set me straight? I had no desire to rehash the matter. Hiroshi is a friend and a black belt at our dojo, so I sucked it up and tried to clarify my position. Things got heated. His daughter, who was passing by, hurried to intervene. I assured her that we weren't fighting, just having a loud discussion. I was serious. Growing up in a family of volatile Italians, where screaming and shouting were the normal mode of communication, I was the polar opposite of the polite, stoic Japanese.

Eugenie walked in on the tail end of things. She took one look at Tanner quivering in his bed and she nailed me with the death stare.

"Check yourself," it said. "If you upset my dog (or this friendship), I WILL hurt you."

I took the hint. I assured Hiroshi that there were no hard feelings, and we said goodbye.

That afternoon, I took Tanner with me to Hiroshi's to apologize. With the dog in tow, I figured there was less chance of me losing it again and reigniting our "debate." When I rang the bell, no one answered. My *mea culpa* would have to wait. As we turned to leave, we met the next-door neighbor, Ian, and his dog, Sketch, a pretty white Pit with a black eye like Petey from *The Little Rascals*. Ian and I shook hands while Tanner and Sketch made friends Pit Bull style, whaling on each other like Ali and Frazier.

Tanner's leash was cramping their play, so I unhooked him. The second I did, Sketch bolted for the complex entrance and Pacific Coast Highway. Tanner followed.

"Come!" I screamed.

He ignored me. My stomach dropped. No way could they survive in the heavy traffic. Then, suddenly, Sketch about-faced and they sprinted back. I slapped the leash on Tanner, and we set off for home. Glancing at the dog trotting beside me, panting hard and covered in slime, I gave a silent prayer of thanks. We'd dodged a terrible bullet and put the morning's bad juju behind us.

When we got in, Tanner went straight to the kitchen and his water dish. I was so engrossed in my recounting of his madcap play-date to Eugenie (to save my hide, I omitted the near-disaster) that I didn't see him flop down on the rug behind me. When I turned to leave, I tripped *Three Stooges*-style. Most dogs would have scooted away. Tanner crouched in terror, waiting for the beating he was sure would follow.

Martial arts training helped me to avoid the glass table and the dog that lay cringing at my feet. In herky-jerky slo-mo, I thudded to the floor. As I lurched to stand, a searing pain flared in my shoulder. I'd spent a year diligently rehabbing a damaged rotator cuff. Now, a freak accident threatened to undo my progress and force me into the painful, costly surgery I'd been hoping to avoid. Worse still, I'd traumatized the dog that we'd been working so hard to heal.

After that, Tanner avoided me big-time. I tried to bribe him with cuddles and extra treats. I lowered my voice to a whisper and curbed my normally emphatic gestures. No matter what happened—if a computer crash deleted an important file, or we got dinged on our healthcare premium, or Eugenie overcooked the rigatoni—I fought to remain serene and non-threatening. It didn't help. Except for walks, when he had no choice, Tanner kept his distance, fearful of another "attack."

Hoping to regain his trust, we paid daily visits to his new love, Sketch, and to his puppy pal, Trouble. Tanner was fine with them, and Eugenie, but he continued to twitch whenever we were alone. The Dog Whisperer, Cesar Millan, says that rehabilitating fearful dogs is much tougher than reprogramming aggressive ones. I could see why. I felt so guilty I'd have given Tanner my bed and served him breakfast in it if that would've set things right between us. It never failed with Eugenie, and I'd had tons of practice!

I was thrown by Tanner's reaction to such a seemingly minor incident. He hadn't been injured, and there'd been no cursing, shouting, or storming about like before I'd started "seeing things differently." Couldn't he tell that I loved him, and that I'd changed, at least a little?

Eugenie offered a surprising and unwelcome explanation. Although I thought that I'd reformed, my energy was still "dark and heavy", she said. It wasn't a question of my actions but of my very self.

"I know you're working hard to improve, and I appreciate it", she told me. "But Tanner doesn't understand that. He's very sensitive. For him, the force of your repressed rage is overwhelming. You're too scary to live with."

I refused to believe it, of course, and blamed the dog for being cowardly and neurotic.

Our estrangement lasted almost a week. Then, as quickly as it had come on, Tanner's PTSD blew over. I went to fetch him for his walk one morning and found him stretched out on the bedroom floor, tail wagging in high spirits like before the "incident." As we rolled around, he kissed my lips and flashed a toothy grin as if to say, "Forget that falling thing; we're good now." I felt relieved, and vindicated.

Shortly after Tanner and I buried the hatchet, we ran into the garage blocker, who was painting the front door of his unit. Instead of scowling and cursing, he greeted us like bosom buddies. He made no mention of our earlier disagreement, and we've been friends ever since.

~~~

I crapped out on *Millionaire,* but Tanner still got new wheels. Thanks to "Cash For Clunkers," I drove off one afternoon in a well-traveled '93 Lexus and returned that evening with a brand new Prius. We debated making it a "dog-free" zone, but that didn't seem fair or fun, so we gradually introduced Tanner to the new car. Like before, he trembled and slobbered. Like before, we stuck close to home, taking only very brief rides. That is, until the Sunday that we drove to Newport Beach to visit Eugenie's godfather.

Call me crazy, but I prefer that "new car" smell to vomit. I voted to leave Tanner home. Despite her soft appearance, Eugenie is a honey badger. She insisted that he come along. She hadn't quit on me, and she wasn't about to bail on Tanner, either, especially after he'd survived the Ventura excursion.

In case he reverted to form, I blanketed the back seat with waterproof pee pads. I stocked our "diaper" bag with essentials—food, treats, and toys—then I went upstairs to shower. While I was gone, Eugenie revised my handiwork. To make things more comfy for Tanner, she had covered the pads with a towel that doubled as his travel bed. I was pissed, and we traded words while Tanner stood drooling beside the car. I should have noticed that he was agitated and ridden in back with him, but I was too caught up in the quarrel. I slid behind the wheel in a huff.

We were approaching Topanga Canyon about ten miles away when he hawked up a small blob of kibble. I pulled over, cleaned up, and got us back on the road. We'd driven only a few more miles when Mt. Tanner erupted again, this time emptying his stomach. Traffic on Coast Highway was heavy, and finding a safe place to stop was tricky. I could have pulled into a private home, but I didn't feel right dumping gallons of vomit on some stranger's driveway, so I headed for the nearest exit.

That's when Eugenie started barking (at least it seemed like barking at the time), "Stop the car! Stop the car! Stop the car!"

Did she think I hadn't noticed the "accident"?!

I stomped the brakes and swerved to the curb. Tanner went sliding across the seat, directly into the mess.

Eugenie was furious. I'd endangered us all and traumatized an already frightened animal. Guilty on both counts, I bit my lip and got to work. When I finished wiping down the dog, I turned my attention to the sea of barf on the seat. I tried to remove the soiled towel, but it wouldn't budge; it was snagged on the seat belt assembly. Exasperated, I jerked it loose, flinging vomit all over the doorframe, the roof liner, and myself.

A dozen baby wipes and half an hour later we finally made it to the freeway. But Tanner wasn't finished. He heaved one last time, dredging up a puddle of nasty yellow bile that soaked through the virgin, now unprotected upholstery.

The drive to Orange County was awful. As we rode in icy silence, I thought of the countless hours I'd spent repairing the damage wrought by my short fuse: the broken dishes, the kicked-in walls, the knuckles scraped bloody from pounding the heavy bag until I'd ripped it from its moorings. And now I had this hypersensitive dog acting as my foil, forcing me to confront my ugly failings.

~~~

*Striding across the lot at Sony Pictures, I'm excited. I'm meeting a heavyweight producer to discuss my latest screenplay, an action saga set in medieval England. He keeps me waiting forever, but that's a given; I'm nobody. Then the phone rings, and the receptionist drifts over. My producer got hung up in a meeting, she tells me sheepishly. I can reschedule or sit down with his assistant, the head of development. I should take the hint and leave. I'm miffed, and so I stay.*

*The woman hasn't read my script. Never will. Period action isn't her "thing." Do I have a thriller, a suspense tale? I do, in fact, and I proceed to give her the log line, the shorthand breakdown of the central idea. When I mention my co-writer, a well-known TV actor and close friend, she glares at me like I'd just fired off the Nazi salute, or said that her dress makes her look* heavy, which it does because she is. "Your friend's a loser!" she snaps. "I would never work with him on anything. Ever!"

I'm thrown, and try to laugh it off, but she keeps coming, cranking up the volume and the venom. "He was engaged to a friend of mine and he really jerked her around. I hate the sonuvabitch! He's a scumbag…a real dick!" That's my exit cue. Or it should be. Instead, I channel my father. I return her stare with a smile. "Well, maybe your friend deserved to get screwed over." Her mouth falls open. "Maybe, she's a total bitch, like you!" I pop up and stroll out.

I'm home five minutes when my agent calls. She's livid. I mention the producer's lame excuse, the assistant's unprovoked, unprofessional attack, but she's not having it. Am I out of my mind?! "Yeah, for thinking you would have my back!" Two bridges torched in less than hour, a banner day, even for me.

~~~

My wife's godfather, Gene, is a Hall of Fame basketball coach who notched more than 800 victories, and one of the nicest, most easygoing people I've ever known. Except for her superior good looks and taste, Jennifer, his wife, is every bit as terrific. It was a gorgeous day and we had brunch outside at a local café, with Tanner curled up beside us, lazing in the sun. If my rash, childish behavior had scarred him further, he was hiding it well.

We spent the afternoon promenading the mall at Fashion Island, where it seemed that every tanned, manicured shopper had a Yorkie or Shih Tzu in tow. We worried about bringing a Pit Bull to staid Orange County, but people constantly stopped us to remark on Tanner's stunning looks and to ask if their dogs could meet him. He soaked it up like a star on the red carpet.

Tanner was fine outdoors where he could waltz right into the stores with us. Then we popped inside to Bloomingdales. As we approached the escalator, his tail dropped, and his gait became hesitant. I didn't give it much thought. He was always wary of new things, and I was still roiling from my earlier meltdown. When we started up, Tanner freaked. He dug in his heels and jerked me backwards, knocking me off my feet. Luckily, Gene was standing behind me and broke my fall. If he hadn't, I'd have toppled headlong down the metal stairs.

All of us were shaken by the close call, me most of all. To regroup, the girls went shopping for shoes. Gene and I retreated to the patio, a haven for shopped-out husbands. We were handicapping college football when a shrill, female voice interrupted.

"Excuse me!"

Across from us, a middle-aged woman sat scowling behind her *Newport Magazine*.

"We don't do that kind of thing here," she said. By "thing" she meant Tanner, who was dozing peacefully on the sofa beside us.

I was caught off guard; it's not uncommon to see dogs on the outdoor furniture, which is covered in all-weather fabric. I could have let it go, should have let it go. Just moments before, the fallout from my tantrum had nearly cost me a trip to the E.R. But her imperious tone bugged me. So, instead of "seeing things differently" and ignoring her, I doubled down.

"Who's *we*?" I asked, glancing around, seemingly perplexed. "All I see is *you*."

She rolled the magazine in her fist. "People from Newport, that's who!" she screeched. "You're obviously not from here."

"Look at you!" I said, glancing down at the Malibu T-shirt I had on. "You're a regular Sherlock Holmes!" Her face flushed. "Well, they sure are lucky to have a mayor like you, keeping us riffraff in line."

She hopped up, jaw set, the veins in her temple bulging. "Wherever you're from, when you leave today, don't come back! We don't want your kind here…you f*cking spic!" With that, she huffed off, cursing under her breath.

I have a foul mouth, especially when I'm hot, yet I was stunned by her vitriol. With no real justification, she had escalated from spirited, harmless repartee (my opinion) to fighting words. In a different setting—a New York City subway or an East L.A. freeway—that casual *spic* might have gotten her slapped, or dead. She was out of line. I was equally guilty. I'd sensed that she was troubled—we later learned that she's a local "character"—but I'd still egged her on and enjoyed it.

Tanner slept the entire way home. When we got in, he wolfed down his supper and took refuge in his bed. The emotional roller coaster had drained me, too. I'd been given several opportunities to practice restraint and botched them all with flying colors. Once again, I'd reverted to my old, negative angry behavior. I'd let my juvenile temper spoil what should have been a fun, relaxing day.

That "progress" that I was so proud of was just a mirage. Eugenie was right, and this time there was no denying it; I *was* too scary to live with. For Tanner. For her. Even for myself.

**With Gene Victor before the run-in with the Newport busybody**

## *THE ODDS OF BEING KILLED BY A PIT BULL*

- ✓ According to Dogsbite.org, an anti-Pit Bull group, as many as 22 dog bite-related fatalities may be attributable to Pit Bulls or Pit Bull mixes. To put that number in perspective:
- ✓ In 2011, the CDC recorded 36,280 deaths from Unintentional Poisoning. 1,650 times the number killed in Pit Bull attacks.
- ✓ That same year, 33,778 people died in Motor Vehicle Accidents, 1,535 times the number killed by Pit Bulls.
- ✓ The CDC notes that approximately 10 people die from drowning every day, the second leading cause of non-intentional death for people ages 1-14. A person is 160 times more likely to drown than to be killed by a Pit bull.
- ✓ In 2011, 1,545 children were killed by their parents or guardians either through abuse or neglect. Those numbers suggest that a child is 70 times more likely to be killed by their caretaker than by a Pit Bull.
- ✓ That year, 53 people died as a result of bee or wasp stings, nearly, more than twice as many as were killed by Pit Bulls.
- ✓ For every Pit Bull that kills, there are MILLIONS that DON'T!

**Resources**

- Centers for Disease Control
- Dogsbite.org
- National Canine Research Council
- Federal Bureau of Investigation

# CHAPTER 9
# SCHOOL DAZE

It's a holiday, Columbus Day, or maybe Veteran's Day, and we're home from school. We can hear them in the kitchen, scrapping about money, gambling, his other women—the usual.

Out late, playing cards or getting laid, the old man's up early, feeling surly, sipping coffee before he heads to "the joint," the restaurant that feeds his habit and steals his soul. She needs money for uniforms. (The public school's a jungle, so we go to the Catholic school across the street.) Does she think it grows on trees?

"Tell it to your Polack whore!"

Before the words have died, he's on her, pushing, slapping, cursing. She grabs a milk bottle from the sink, bangs him in the head, but he keeps coming

My brother and I rush in. Young men now (at least in our minds) with bulging biceps and raging hormones, we pry them apart. "Go for her again and you come through us!" He leaves without a word. I'm surprised and strangely disappointed.

**Training at Malibu Dog Park**

My Newport meltdown took me back twenty-five years, to New York City and the night that I pummeled a pair of fare-beaters who had dared to rip me off. When other cabbies heard my tale, they cheered me as a hero, heartened that some poor working slob would actually fight back. I knew better. Yeah, the deadbeats had done me wrong and deserved to pay for it. But my Travis Bickle stand was about more than money. It was about a stalled acting career, a foundering romance, and my fragile ego, the products of years of self-loathing. Like that incident, this latest eruption was merely a symptom of something bigger and more pernicious, not the cause. For that, I'd have to look inside.

I didn't see the point. *The Course* had promised "miracles" but what had it gotten me? I'd spent several months working to understand my jumbled feelings and transform my life to no avail. I was as reactive as ever. If anything, I felt worse than before for having tried and failed. Miracles, my ass! I had better things to do with my Tuesday nights. I'd go back to karate. Or watch football. Or do sudoku. Anything was preferable to this. Eugenie and Tanner would have to deal with me the way I was. Or not. I was finished with "self-improvement."

~~~

At that week's class, I shamefully recounted my debacle. Ed merely smiled and thanked me for sharing my spectacular screw-up. Personal transformation wasn't about forgiving my dog for messing the car or a nosy woman for offering an unsolicited opinion, he patiently explained. It was about letting go of old, destructive patterns and forgiving my own shortcomings and mistakes.

As long as I was still at war with myself—a brutal conflict I'd been waging since my teens—I'd continue to rage at the world around me. I couldn't control the world and force others to change, although God knows I'd tried. But, maybe, if I worked real hard, I might control myself. Ed said to relax, that slipping up was a necessary part of the process. There would be plenty of opportunities to improve. Would there ever.

Later that week, I took Tanner to the vet for a checkup. For a change, he seemed relaxed in the car, almost happy. As we pulled into the parking lot he yawned and let fly. I cheerfully (okay, I wasn't exactly cheerful but I didn't go ballistic) scooped out the barf, wiped his mug, and steered him inside. Dr. Lisa was impressed; Tanner looked great, and he'd gained five pounds since his April reading. She administered his booster shots, then I paid the bill, and we jogged across the road to the deli for lunch.

The outdoor tables were full, so I secured him to a heavy wooden love seat while I went inside to order. I never imagined that there might be a problem. In New York, we always left our dogs tied up outside. As I entered the restaurant, a young woman started down the stairs carrying a tray of food. She lost her balance and the tray went flying. So did Tanner, who dove down the steps, dragging the love seat with him like it was made of cardboard.

As I lugged the bench back into place, I passed a man in a car talking on his cell phone. He was glaring at me, shaking his head. I couldn't hear what he was saying, so I motioned for him to lower the window and repeat himself. He mumbled that I was "...reckless and irresponsible, leaving a vicious dog to attack that poor girl."

Grrr! I could feel my bad self clawing to get out. I took a breath and thought of Tanner, Ed and *The Course*.

For two days running, I'd slipped back into my old, comfortable groove, worn deep with time and practice, of raging against external forces that "made" me angry—my wife, the Newport busybody, the car witness. Standing there, eyeing my accuser, I saw that, in each instance, I was really angry with myself for failing to recognize or prevent a potential problem. And then, when the puke hit the fan, instead of taking responsibility for my part in the commotion, I spewed my venom, and the blame, on someone else.

I sent Angry Lou back to the basement and addressed the man in the car. Instead of blasting him with profanity, I calmly explained that he was mistaken. Tanner hadn't attacked anyone. My terrified dog was merely reacting to a perceived threat by trying to escape. Had he actually witnessed the "attack", or had he simply filled in the blanks when the girl's shout interrupted his call and he saw that Tanner was a Pit Bull? He looked away, busted, and drove off.

I was pleased that I'd checked myself but concerned about Tanner's wild reaction and his persistent vomiting. When we got home, I called Rob Lerner, who recommended that we take a different approach in dealing with the car. Instead of avoiding it or gritting our teeth and hoping for the best like we'd been doing, he suggested we shift the energy by taking Tanner out at least once a day, every day, to fun places like Carl's house, the park, or the beach. To speed things along, we could also try feeding him inside the car, to create a positive association with it.

At dinnertime, we filled his bowl with kibble, waved it under his nose, and led him down to the garage. Tanner has a hearty appetite. When we set his dish on the car seat, he looked at us like we'd gone mad and darted back upstairs. We were disappointed and surprised; most dogs are food whores that will whine, beg, and literally jump through hoops for the tiniest morsel.

For fourteen years, our "Dalmatian From Hell" badgered us at every meal, swiping any grub left unattended. Meat, poultry, fish, fruit—anything was fair game. Roxanne once pilfered the ingredients for a batch of cookies—two sticks of butter, a pound of sugar, and an entire package of chocolate chips—-devouring everything including the paper wrappers and plastic bag. Chocolate can prove fatal to pets. Except for a scary burst of hyperactivity (she was literally bouncing off the walls) and a killer case of the doggie farts, Rox escaped unscathed.

Roxanne was a handful, but it wasn't all her fault. Rebel was there when Eugenie and I were just beginning our romance, during that halcyon time of long walks, candlelight picnics, and steamy evenings making love. We were ecstatic and so was he. By the time we got Roxanne, we were foundering and scrapping daily. She was a testament to our dysfunction.

In passing, Eugenie had mentioned that she "loved" Dalmatians. My grandparents once had a Dalmatian, a loony dog named Smitty that chased after women in hats and tore up the furniture when left alone. I should have known better.

I ignored history. I called around and found a breeder that was selling a recent litter. We drove to Upstate New York to view the pups, a dozen adorable, fur-covered dice. According to the gracious breeder, we were free to choose whichever one we liked, except for one breathtakingly gorgeous female that he intended to show. Naturally, we picked her.

Unlike gluttonous Roxanne, Rebel had to be coaxed into sampling even gourmet human fare. He was tall but carried a measly seventy-five pounds on his wiry frame, prompting friends and strangers to accuse us of starving him. We tried all sorts of premium dog foods, even adding gravy and leftovers to his meals.

Nothing piqued his interest. I'd stir his food, begging him to try "just one more bite." He'd take a few nibbles. Then he'd gaze up at me, tail swishing happily, waiting to be excused so we could play. It was the dog equivalent of Slow Dining and the pattern never changed.

Once, early on, I skipped the kibble and shared my spaghetti Bolognese. Reb gobbled it down. I went off to the gym thrilled I'd solved the problem. When I stepped off the elevator a few hours later, a vicious stench smacked me between the eyes. I entered the apartment to find my beige carpet spattered with reddish-brown pools of foul-smelling liquid. Blood!

Thinking he'd ingested rat poison or some other lethal toxin, I rushed him to our vet, a gentle, commonsensical man who, with his bald head, bushy mustache, and multiple earrings, resembled an urbane pirate. He checked the dog and asked about Reb's diet, if I'd given him anything unusual.

"No," I replied. "Just dog food…and pasta with meat sauce."

Jolly Roger smiled, handed me the bill, and said to stick with kibble.

Evade, block, counter. Evade, block, counter. Evade, block, counter. In karate, you practice the basics thousands of times until they become ingrained in your "muscle memory." Once you've cut the groove and removed thought from the equation, response is automatic. That's why correctness of form is essential. Pick up a bad habit early on, like a weak kick or sloppy footwork, and you can spend years trying to undo it.

React, attack, destroy. React, attack, destroy. React, attack, destroy.

***The writer, Eugenie, Rebel, and
"The Dalmatian From Hell" - Madison Park, NYC, 1990***

Through decades of diligent practice, I had acquired the mother of bad habits. I'd arrogantly underestimated the depth of my rage and the enormity of the task at hand. Now I was paying the price.

Terrible as it was, the Newport disaster proved to be a turning point in my furious, and so far futile, struggle for emotional sanity. Having hit bottom, or as close as I ever wanted to go, I rededicated myself to doing whatever it took to become a better, kinder man and dog owner. Using my deli triumph as a springboard, I diligently tackled the CIM workbook and investigated other "groovy" works like *The Untethered Soul, The Anatomy of Peace,* and the writings of Pema Chodron, a renowned Buddhist teacher and former housewife, Her no-nonsense, upbeat, humorous approach gave me hope that even a chronic rage-aholic like me might eventually "get it."

Despite my concerted efforts, progress was brutally choppy. Some days I was the Dalai Lama; others I was Mike Tyson. Most of the time I was Jekyll and Hyde, a tortured creature of manic moods swings, careening from sunny to surly, and back again, in the blink of an eye. My moorings had been cut, and I was adrift between an old, fearful place and a new uncertain one.

There was no blinding epiphany for me, no single knockout blow. It was trench warfare, battling my demons for a tiny swath of emotional turf, struggling to hold it, and then hopefully advancing toward the far-distant goal. The process was daunting, but there was no turning back. Even if I'd wanted to, the transformation was too far along. I would have to ride it out.

Watching my jarring roller coaster ride, Eugenie was moved and impressed. Nevertheless, she wondered why a brief, tenuous relationship with a rescue dog, even one as sweet and loveable as Tanner, would inspire me to undertake such a difficult transformation when my human connections, including my twenty-year marriage to the woman I adore, had failed to move me to action.

A therapist I know offered an interesting theory. Unlike family and friends, Tanner was ignorant of my positive qualities (you're probably shocked, but there are a few). He, therefore, couldn't use them to excuse my constant outbursts. Ours was a simple "yes" or "no" relationship: he either felt safe with me, or he didn't. Being non-verbal, he couldn't engage me in ways that might trigger the very dynamic I was trying to correct. He was merely a furry, four-legged looking glass, reflecting back to me my brooding, ugly self, a self I could no longer ignore.

~~~

Amazingly, as I calmed down, so did Tanner. At bedtime he raced downstairs, happy just to snore beside us. In the morning, he licked our sleepy faces, thrilled to see that we hadn't run off while he slept. From day one, we'd vowed to keep him off the furniture. That resolve was crumbling, especially when he stood on his hind legs, forepaws resting on our mattress, being extra cute and wiggly the way dogs are when they're hoping to skirt the rules. He seemed happier than ever, as if by sharing our room we'd proven that he really belonged with us, that this was, indeed, his home.

Returning from our walks, he would rocket upstairs into the kitchen, his muscular legs churning in place like the cartoon roadrunner. He'd devour his kibble, and, most days a spoonful of yogurt. Then it was time for his chew stick. Perching anxiously beside Eugenie's chair, he'd stay until she asked for a "kiss," which looked like a head butt from Hulk Hogan. If we were lucky, the rawhide bought us a few minutes to wolf down our coffee and oatmeal before breaking out the toys.

A hand-written note in Tanner's shelter file says, "Loves to play." The first few months, when all he did was cringe and flinch, we were sure we'd been *Punk'd* by wiseass volunteers who'd conned us into adopting the least playful dog on the planet. Now he was frisking about like a wild colt that had taken to nibbling locoweed.

Tanner had finally hoisted his freak flag. Curing his auto-phobia proved to be slower sailing. The puking had nearly ceased, but he still distrusted the car. He's an incredibly athletic dog—he can maneuver like Messi, run like Usain Bolt, and jump like Blake Griffin—yet he approached the rear seat like an octogenarian tackling Mt. Everest. On a good day, it took a minute for him to make the climb. On a bad day, you could finish *Moby Dick* before he reached the summit.

We cheered, cajoled, and bribed him with food like Rob suggested. Nothing worked to calm his dread. Whether we were going to the corner, or Santa Barbara, I always rode in back with him. You couldn't tell, because he would lie scrunched down, out of sight. Even in offbeat Malibu it must've looked bizarre to see a gorgeous redhead chauffeuring an eccentric dude around town in a Prius. My neighbors probably just assumed I'd been busted for DUI.

~~~

For some strange reason, Tanner was drawn to gates. In my imagination, I see him as a terrified pup making like Steve McQueen in *The Great Escape*, nosing the latch and slipping away from his former, abusive owners. If my theory is true, then gates meant freedom and adventure. More likely, he was just a very nosy dog.

A rusted metal gate separates our complex from the church and school next door. As we strolled by each morning, he'd dig in his heels and tug me toward it. It's private property, and most days there were kids around, so I'd tell him "no" and nudge him along in the opposite direction. It was summer now and school was out, and so I finally gave in and indulged his curiosity.

Tanner was over the moon. He bounced along giddily, stopping every few feet to water his new turf...until we reached the chicken coop. The homemade wire pen held a jaunty rooster and a few hens, Rhode Island whites, most likely the product of a science classroom incubator. One peek at the strange-looking clucksters, all sharp beaks and scratchy claws, and Tanner pulled up quaking; Shangri-la had become a nightmare. I offered to let him investigate further but he'd seen enough and dragged me back to the gate.

Tanner was chicken with chickens yet, since his showdown with the coyote, he'd become a formidable watchdog. He barked if anyone came to the door or dared "sneak up" from behind when we were out walking. He was especially protective of Eugenie, whom he considered his equal in our pack. One evening when I was away, they happened upon some rowdy (drunken?) college students that were carousing outside of our place. Tanner didn't like it. He puffed out his chest and made like Cujo. They got the message and took the party elsewhere.

He stood guard inside the house as well. I was reading in bed one night when, for no apparent reason, he started growling. Straining my ears, I caught a faint, high-pitched squeal coming from the next room. Some wild animal had breached our perimeter. As the black-belt wearing alpha dog, it was on me to deal with it. I threw on my shoes, screwed up my courage, and tiptoed into the office, ready to face down the monster. But there were no rabid raccoons, or feral ferrets, only my wife, sitting red-faced at the computer. The "beast" was just a gnarly case of indigestion from a spicy taco lunch. I ordered Tanner to stand down, and went back to my book.

~~~

Now that we'd opened Pandora's box (or, in his case, gate), Tanner insisted on visiting the verboten churchyard every morning. Blithely ignoring the "No Trespassing" sign, we would slip inside and roam the grounds, taking pains to avoid the caretaker and the poultry. After the beach, it was Tanner's favorite spot. For me, our complex with its gossipy neighbors and plethora of dogs was far more interesting. Just like with people, there's no accounting for dog taste.

Early one Saturday morning, Tanner had just finished soiling holy ground when a gaggle of neighborhood kids cycled by with their dogs in tow. Tanner raced to join them while I fought to keep him from demolishing the caravan and sending them all to the E.R. The Dog Whisperer, Cesar Millan, often bikes with rowdy dogs as part of their therapy. No matter how unruly or headstrong the mutts, they always trot docilely beside him, never stopping to mark, or chase squirrels, or capriciously veer off course like they do for the rest of us.

Through an odd twist of fate, Tanner nearly met the man himself. The previous year, friends had invited us to a fund-raising auction for a local charity. Cesar was a guest of honor, having donated a puppy that he'd personally trained, as well as a private, two-hour session. The pup, a fluffy little poodle, went for somewhere north of $7K. Bidding on the training opened at a grand and quickly soared to five...ten...fifteen thousand dollars as our friends and a Beverly Hills matron traded blows like gladiators. When the tally reached $20,000, the auctioneer called the battle a draw, and Cesar generously donated two sessions.

Our friends' dog was the intended trainee. When a year passed and they hadn't cashed the marker, they asked if we'd like Cesar's help in dealing with Tanner's car phobia and his overly enthusiastic play. We jumped at the chance. If anyone could get Tanner to like the car, it was Cesar. Unfortunately, due to scheduling issues, the lesson never happened. We forgot all about it until the day we ran into Bonnie and Winnie by the pool.

Tanner had just finished tussling with Sketch. He was seriously riled up, charging about like a wounded rhino. In his delirium, he slammed into Bonnie's thigh, leaving a nasty mango-sized bruise.

"It's no big deal," she said, gritting her teeth. "It's just nice to see him so happy."

That night, he lunged to greet a neighbor's Westie and dragged Eugenie down a flight of stairs. She escaped with only a twisted ankle. Early next morning, we enrolled Tanner in dog obedience class.

~~~

We started school at Bluffs Park on a Thursday night in mid-September, without Tanner. The trainer, Tony Rollins, ordered the class to leave our dogs at home so that he could outline his philosophy, which called for us to assume the "alpha" role. Since alpha dogs don't bribe their packs, using treats was forbidden. For homework, we were to practice "sit" and "come" for twenty minutes a day. Tony underlined the importance of teaching your dog to "come." In the case of traffic, bears, or rattlesnakes, it could well save his life.

"If your dog won't 'come' on command," he told us, "you're not really the owner, just the person who feeds him."

Tanner joined us the following week. It was a hot, sultry evening. He moped around until he saw his classmates, a dozen dogs of all sizes and breeds including a Great Dane pup and a young Rottweiler. We worried that other owners might freak at the sight of a Pit Bull, so we were thrilled he wasn't the only dominant breed dog.

We spent the hour practicing "heel," keeping Tanner on our left, making sharp right turns whenever he lagged or strayed off course. He was perplexed by our suddenly stern attitude, annoyed that we wouldn't let him romp with all those new, furry friends.

If we had any doubts about Tony's method, he quickly put them to rest with two Brittany Spaniel brothers. Before class, they'd never ridden in a car or even been out of the house. They were predictably crazed, tugging and bellowing like steers being led to the slaughter. After five minutes with Tony, they were meek as kittens and almost obedient.

To enhance the training, Tony urged us to use a prong or pinch collar. He said it would make for faster correction than a regular choker, at the same time placing less pressure on Tanner's throat.

We took his advice, and Tanner's walking improved dramatically, but the collar irritated his skin. We felt guilty, as Tony had cautioned we would. He suggested removing a few links to make it fit more snuggly and prevent chafing. When we tried that, however, we couldn't slip it over Tanner's huge head. There was a simple solution. Space cadets that we are, it never dawned on us.

Tanner's second week of school was a humbling experience…for us. When Eugenie walked him for Tony, Tanner did pretty much as he pleased, stopping constantly to sniff or dragging her around the field to get at the other dogs that were behaving just as badly. Since we were forbidden to ply him with treats, he even managed to screw up "sit" and "down," the only parts of his repertoire he'd sort of mastered.

While the dogs took a breather, Tony showed the owners how to properly fasten the collar. A prong or pinch collar consists of multiple links of steel chain, each with blunted prongs that pinch the dog's neck whenever the owner tugs the leash to correct him. It looks like S & M gear, but it's easier on the dog than a choke or slip collar which, in unskilled hands, often leaves the animal gasping for air.

To remove the collar, you simply unhook one of the links. To fasten it, you reconnect the ends. It's so obvious and simple a child can do it. Unfortunately for Tanner, his owners aren't smarter than a fifth grader. We'd struggled to slip the barbed crown over his massive dome the way we'd done with Rebel, whose face was much longer and narrower.

Like so many things, including my anger, it was more a matter of perspective than knowledge. Had we stopped to really consider the situation and think outside our misguided box, we'd have found the answer in minutes instead of years. Judging from the first two classes, it was going to be a long, challenging course for all of us.

~~~

For Tanner's six-month anniversary we had planned a joyous celebration with toys, treats, and a romp on the beach. A rare fall storm hit before dawn, and I had to pry him from his bed just to get him out the door. To buck him up, I told him how Rebel loved the nasty New York winters and how Blanche, our cat, would beg to go outside in a gale to lap up dirty rainwater. He didn't care.

He looked so miserable that I cut short our walk. We returned home, drenched. His bowels and bladder were as full as when we left. He spurned his breakfast and parked himself under the table. He wanted nothing to do with his toys. By noon, he was looking ill at ease and passing wind. The time for coddling was over. I hauled him outside into the elements, where we splashed around until he finally gave it up.

The showers spilled over to the next day, which was our anniversary. Rain seemed fitting: we were married in a downpour on October 14, 1988, in Verona, Italy. We spent the night before floating down the Grand Canal in Venice, with strains of Italian love songs echoing off centuries-old palazzi. It was a magical moment worthy of Romeo and Juliet.

The follow morning we awoke to a deluge. We donned our wedding finery and hauled our suitcases to the water taxi that would take us to the station. The rush hour train was so packed with wet businessmen that we were forced to ride to our nuptials in separate cars. When we reached Verona, we dragged our luggage through the pouring rain to City Hall. We looked like waterlogged refugees.

At the Ufficio di Matrimonio, the clerk peppered me in machine gun Italian. I had no idea what she was saying, but her frantic gestures were unmistakable: I'd screwed up the paperwork. If it had been New York or Berlin, they'd have sent us packing with a shrug. The Veronese were more forgiving. They were flattered that we'd chosen their city for our wedding. They marched us down to Juliet's Tomb where the Mayor donned his official red, white, and green sash and joined us in holy wedlock.

*The writer and Eugenie, Verona, Italy, 1988*

As he pronounced us man and wife, he glanced outside at the driving rain. He smiled and prophesied our union would be blessed.

"Spoza bagnata, spoza fortunata," he said. "A wet bride is a lucky bride."

To celebrate our continuing good fortune, we'd booked a trip to Solvang, a town just north of Santa Barbara in the heart of wine country, made famous (infamous, if you ask the locals) by the movie *Sideways*.

It was to be our first overnighter with Tanner. With the forecast calling for more storms, a long drive in foul weather with a queasy dog seemed like a recipe for disaster. We reluctantly postponed.

For the next week, it rained buckets. Tanner fussed on every walk, stepping gingerly to avoid the sodden ground. Like a Secret Service detail, we flanked him with our umbrellas, ensuring that his coat stayed dry while we got soaked. If the odd drop eluded us, we toweled him off and swaddled him like a newborn infant. As the rainy days dragged on, he sulked in his bed, staring mournfully at the lowering clouds as if we'd purposely arranged the dingy conditions.

Fortunately, the sun returned in time for our rescheduled trip. With Tanner perched on my lap in back, his head draped out the window like a normal dog, we wound our way up the coast. He'd linger for a minute, sniffing intensely, then execute a slow U-turn, wiping drool on my cheek while stomping on my bladder like a punk rocker at CBGB. The Prius was barely three months old, yet it looked like we'd had it forever. There were towels, pee pads, and toys scattered everywhere. You'd have thought we were raising a brood of rambunctious toddlers.

Billed "The Danish Capital of America", Solvang is renowned for its quaint, European-style architecture and decadent bakeries. The intoxicating aroma of butter-laden pastries is so thick you could blow a diet just by breathing. The bear claws were tempting, but our first stop was the pet store where we bought Tanner a fancy nylon collar to replace the one that he'd inherited from Reggie. He seemed grateful for the new bling. With a bounce in his step, he led us to The Wandering Dog café and wine bar. The place looked inviting, and we were parched from the long drive. I asked the owner if Tanner could join us on the patio.

"Absolutely not," he said. "He'll drink inside with the rest of us."

And so he did, sipping water and munching doggie donuts while we sampled the local grape.

As we sauntered down the main drag to Eugenie's favorite stores, female shoppers constantly stopped us to coo over the dog with the "big, beautiful eyes." Watching Tanner pose and preen I wondered if, perhaps, we shouldn't have given him a more apt name, like maybe Leo, or George, or Brad.

There were still ten weeks to go, but Eugenie was anxious to finish her Christmas shopping. She's always prompt, sometimes painfully so. On numerous occasions we've arrived for dinner parties only to find our flustered hosts in various states of undress, never having imagined that civilized guests would actually show up on time.

Her punctuality was reinforced by her stint in New York, where she had a successful practice giving shiatsu massage to the city's movers and shakers. For ten years, she booked as many as eight appointments a day, six days a week, and was rarely, if ever, tardy. She couldn't afford to be since New Yorkers guard their time the way Malibu surfers police the local breaks. Come huffing in two minutes late, drenched in sweat, and the disgruntled client would frown and tap his Patek Phillipe. Run over by a cab? Mugged in the subway? Caught in a bank heist? "Not my problem; we've got a schedule to keep here!" Eugenie brings the same attitude to Christmas shopping, aiming to have it wrapped up by Halloween.

Back at the hotel, we waited until Tanner fell asleep, then we slipped out to a new restaurant run by the Chumash Indians who also own the nearby casino. We hastily put away oysters, burgers, and a bottle of local pinot noir. We skipped dessert, paid our tab, and hurried back to check on the "baby." Door-to-door, we were gone fifty-five minutes.

Even before Tanner we were always brisk diners. Years ago, on one of our annual Cape Cod getaways, we visited a romantic, Provincetown bistro. With Moroccan-style beaded curtains, private booths and sensuous music, "Franco's Hideaway" was a charming room, the perfect place to ignite a steamy affair or spice up a cooled-down marriage.

We had a delicious three-course dinner. When I asked for the bill, the maitre D' hurried over.

"Was everything all right, sir?" he asked nervously.

"It was terrific. Why?"

He cleared his throat. "It's been barely an hour," he said, glancing at his watch. "Most of our guests stay two or three."

Eugenie assured him that we loved the place and would linger next time. "Right now, we're going home to fool around."

Thankfully, some things never change.

The next morning, we left Tanner guarding the car while we toured the Quick Silver miniature horse ranch. Unlike Shetland ponies with their stumpy legs, the diminutive creatures are properly proportioned horses, only much smaller, like thoroughbreds left too long in the dryer. Originally bred as draught animals, they're a blast to watch; especially the babies who will romp balls-out and then collapse in a heap like they've been hit with a tranquilizer dart.

To reward Tanner's fortitude in dealing with life on the road, we dropped by the pet shop for new toys, including a stuffed hedgehog with sixteen ear-piercing squeakers. Then we loaded the car, settled our tab, and drove home. That evening, he trudged upstairs so fatigued that he could barely lift his tail. We didn't have the heart to tell him that we'd be leaving for school within the hour.

During the first two sessions, Tanner hadn't received much attention from the teacher. That night he got the spotlight. We were practicing "come" when he broke ranks and bolted after one of the other pups, a fetching little Poodle named Poppyseed.

Tony snatched the recall leash from me. "Nnnooo Dog!...Nnnooo Dog!...Nnnooo Dog!" he shouted as he jerked Tanner into submission.

Like most husbands, Tanner's memory was spotty. It took a dozen tries before he got the hang of it. Every time he strayed,

Tony reeled him in like a thrashing marlin. By the end of class, Tanner was spent. Long before lights out, he flopped down on his bed, eyes slammed shut, dead to the world.

Tanner came home from Solvang with a new collar, new toys, and a persistent, rattling cough. His girlfriend, Sketch, also had one and we worried that perhaps he'd contracted an STD—a sniffing transmitted disease. Dr. Lisa diagnosed it as an upper respiratory infection. She prescribed antibiotic pills that Eugenie delivered in leftover steak. Tanner was easily and gladly hoodwinked.

Such a crude gambit would never have fooled Dudley. Whenever we tried to dose him, the little bugger would hold the food in his mouth, sifting it like an old prospector until he'd found and ejected the tiniest sliver of medicine. The crafty black Pug was a birthday gift from Eugenie to her mom. A free spirit with friends all over the country, Melissa worried that a dog might cramp her footloose style. To allay her fears, we promised to baby-sit when she got the urge to ramble. We wound up sharing custody for more than a decade until Reggie came along.

~~~

On our second date, Eugenie and I went to the Greenwich Village Halloween Parade dressed as Tarzan and Jane. Rebel was Cheetah. This year, Eugenie was Cat Woman in leopard tights, black felt ears, and a long velvet tail. I was a priest gone bad—an easy stretch for me—in a cheap, polyester cassock and gold-plated cross. Tanner was a carsick Pit Bull with a skull bandana.

We went trick-or-treating in the Colony, where they do Halloween Hollywood-style. Resident movie stars, studio bosses, and other showbiz big wigs pull out all the stops, hiring FX pros to create a phantasmagoria of gore and mayhem to rival a major theme park. There were flying bats, howling werewolves, and creepy vampires rising from the grave. One twisted neighbor stuffed the chest of a prop ghoul with hotdogs and sausage.

Tanner can be fainthearted, but he coolly strode the gauntlet of menacing ghouls and rotting zombies. As we approached the cul-de-sac, he stopped to relieve himself and was ambushed by a pair of shrieking Yorkies in tiny pink tutus. Their owner turned away, horrified, certain that her ballerinas would meet a grisly end. But Tanner didn't dismember the nervy little rats, or even growl. He was too busy backpedaling, looking for a safe place to finish going. The woman scooped up her babies and ran off.

Afterwards, Eugenie observed, "Poor Tanner's like Frankenstein's monster. He just wants to make friends but he ends up scaring the hell out of people."

With Halloween came the end of Daylight Savings Time. Tanner didn't mind, but I was bummed. Ever since I was a kid playing hoops in the schoolyard till the last shred of light, I've hated the time change. Darkness has its advantages, and even makes sense, in places like work-driven New York, where the residents look harried and the buildings grimy during daylight hours. Once old Sol goes nighty-night, however, and the shimmering lights come up, the City takes on a magical glow. Freed from their desks and cubicles, put-upon Manhattanites retreat to theatres, museums, and restaurants where they actually look...happy.

It's different in California, the land of Endless Summer, where diehard surfers, hikers, and bikers relish the outdoors the way the Italians savor racy sports cars. Mandating premature darkness and forcing them inside where they're stuck watching reruns of *Gossip Girl* is just plain wrong. If the Golden State ever mounts a secession movement, the time change will be its rallying cry.

The early darkness wreaked havoc with my circadian rhythm and with Tanner's schooling as well. Thanks to the time shift, the final two classes were moved from the soccer field to the lighted parking lot. The penultimate week, I had been teaching tai chi and arrived late. The dogs were lined up on the blacktop and told to "Stay" until called. Tanner was distracted and kept breaking ranks to chase after his classmates. Eugenie grew exasperated trying to restrain him, and so I offered to step in.

Tanner had been in school for six weeks. In that time he'd really mastered only one command, "Go to place." Whenever we practiced on our own, he'd hurry to his mat and stay "Down" until we came to get him. When Tony asked for a volunteer, I jumped in, eager to let my dog redeem himself. Tony threw us a change-up. He had me drop the leash, then give the order. Since we'd always escorted Tanner to "place," he did exactly what you'd expect. Nothing. It was Tony's way of telling us that, while we'd made some progress, we'd barely scratched the surface. I felt bad for Tanner, and for us. We'd put in a lot of hard work but it didn't show.

With one class remaining, we redoubled our efforts. We practiced on every walk and put in extra time at the Farm before *The Course*. That Thursday, before the final class, Eugenie drove down early to the park and ran Tanner through his paces. "Sit." "Down." "Stay." "Place." He nailed them all and even came when called. He was right as rain and ready to go.

Like the previous time, Tony tweaked the rules to confound us. Instead of "Heel," he had us walk our dogs without holding the leash. That sounds easy enough, but the Coast Highway with its four lanes of traffic runs right by the park. If Tanner bolted and made it through the hedges surrounding the lot, the result would be disastrous.

Eugenie was afraid to risk it. She handed me the reins. I looked at the cars flashing by, then down at Tanner, so alert and eager to please.

"Trust your dog," Tony always said. I took a long breath, dropped the leash, and strode away.

"Heel," I called. Tanner hesitated for a beat, then fell in beside me, so focused on the job at hand that he never even glanced at the road.

After class, Tony took us aside. Tanner had impressed him. Not only was he sweet and handsome, he was also smart. Our dog had made great strides. So had I. The time spent practicing together had helped me cultivate the patience that I was sorely lacking. It had deepened our bond and earned me Tanner's trust. Tony claimed that he's never had a dog graduate to Level II

Obedience. We told him we were aiming to be the first, and to help change the breed's undeserved reputation.

Even if Tanner never becomes the Pit Bull poster boy, he's already made a difference for at least one other dog. Hearing Carl sing Tanner's praises, his son, Eric, went out and rescued a handsome gray Pit named Dutch from the shelter only hours before he was due to be put down.

***Dutch and Tanner***

# FINDING A DOG TRAINER

If your dog displays unwanted behavior—barking, biting, carsickness, aggression towards other animals or humans, separation anxiety, or overly rough play—first check with your veterinarian to make sure the animal isn't sick or injured. This is especially important for well-behaved older dogs that suddenly develop issues like soiling the house. Once your vet rules out health problems, you might want to get help from a qualified trainer, behaviorist, or a veterinarian with behavioral training.

**Professional Help**

Trainers: Education, hands-on experience and methods can vary greatly from trainer to trainer. "Certified" trainers should be recognized by an independent body, not merely by a school or program they paid to attend.

The Association of Professional Dog Trainers (ADPT) offers certification through the Certification Council for Profession Dog Trainers. Requirements include a specified number of hours of hands-on training experience, references, and a standardized test that covers knowledge of canine behavior and teaching skills. The CCPDT, www.ccpdt.org, offers a list of certified dog trainers.

Behaviorists: Certified Applied Animal Behaviorists (CAABs) and Associate Applied Animal Behaviorists (ACAABs) are professionals with supervised graduate training in animal behavior, biology, and zoology at accredited universities. As experts with both academic and hands-on knowledge, they can determine how and why your pet's behavior is abnormal and help teach you how to alter the unwanted behavior.

Many behaviorists are familiar with common medical issues, and psychotropic medications, like tranquilizers and antidepressants, that your vet might recommend. For a list of behaviorists, visit www.certifiedanimalbehaviorists.com.

Veterinarians with Behavioral Training: Some CAABs are veterinarians who have completed a residency in animal behavior and earned certification from the American College of Veterinary Behaviorists. To become a Diplomat of the ACVB, they must complete a residency and pass a qualifying exam.

**Training Options**

Group Obedience Classes: Many cities offer basic obedience classes through their Parks and Recreation Departments. Group sessions are great for puppy socialization, correcting minor problems and instilling basic obedience. While cheaper than private sessions or board-and-train facilities, they offer less one-on-one attention.

Private Sessions: Some behavioral problems—like aggression, separation anxiety, destructive behavior or phobias—are beyond the scope of a group class. In those cases, your dog might need more intensive, individual attention from a qualified professional.

Day Training: The trainer or behaviorist will work with your dog at your home or his facility to instill desired behaviors or eliminate unwanted ones like barking, chewing and aggression.

Board-and-Train: Some trainers and boarding facilities offer resident training for people who lack the time or desire to train their dogs. It's important that the trainer also work with the dog's guardians to reinforce the lessons.

**Before Committing to a Trainer or Training Facility**
- ✓ Ask your veterinarian and fellow dog owners for recommendations.
- ✓ Interview several trainers or facilities. In addition to comparing prices, inquire about their methods, training and experience.
- ✓ Ask for client references. Cross off any trainer who refuses to provide them.
- ✓ If you are considering group training, ask to monitor a class before signing up.
- ✓ Consider trainers who treat you and your dog with respect, who reward positive behavior, and avoid those who prefer aversion and intimidation.

**Resources**
- Certified Council For Professional Dog Trainers
- Certified Applied Animal Behaviorists
- ASPCA, "Finding Professional Help"
- Rob Lerner, CPDT-KSA
- Tony Rollins, Tony Rollins K-9 Academy

# CHAPTER 10
# REDEMPTION

*We're slouched at the cramped kitchen table, heavy-lidded, my oldest sister, my brother, and me, shoveling in bacon and eggs while my mother packs our lunches by the sink. In the distance, the foyer door slams. My father is back from another all-nighter, shooting craps, or playing ziganette, or clubbing with his girlfriend. He'll crash for a few hours, then rush off to the madness that's the family restaurant and his ticket to the good life.*

*Like a crazed football coach, she huddles us together, waiting for our cue. He enters, and she gives us the nod.*

*Our drowsy morning voices croak, "Daddy, dear old daddy, you've been more than a father to me…"—a Depression era ditty about a selfless dad who sacrifices all for his children.*

*There's no gusto from us. We know it's wrong, but we owe her so we play our part.*

*The pain in her smile…the malice in his eyes…hard to believe they once loved each other.*

~~~

Tanner had "graduated" summa cum laude but we continued our daily training, working to hone his hard-earned repertoire and strengthen our connection. As gangs of surly crows hectored us to steer clear of their nest, we reviewed the basics on our morning walks To challenge Tanner, I kept adding new wrinkles, like letting him carry his babies door-to-door, showing him how to trot beside me without the leash, and teaching him to perch on the koi pond bench without diving for sushi.

For a recovering night owl, those early jaunts well could have been torture. Like most things, including my anger, it was a matter of perspective. Instead of sleeping in and lingering over coffee with the NBA box scores, hitting the pavement with Tanner offered time for reflection and a chance to bond with him, to experience life through his bright, inquisitive eyes.

There was no listening to music, yakking on the phone, or checking e-mail; I had the rest of the day for that. The walk was our time; just the two of us exploring the neighborhood, wondering who and what we'd see that day. The route seldom varied, and it was usually the same faces: Dexter, Ceba, Winnie, Otto, Trouble, and Sketch. Sometimes we'd meet a new dog or chat up a new neighbor. If we were extra lucky, we might chance upon the rabbits, herons, hawks, and deer that call the mountains home.

These peaceful strolls were a far cry from New York and my walks with Rebel. Morning and night, those streets throbbed with the energy of eight million bustling souls leaving their mark on the Naked City. Every trip meant seven flights of stairs, or waiting for the elevator and a possible scuffle with one of the hulking Shepherds, Akitas, and Dobermans that called our building home. For fun, we had the parks. There was Washington Square, where Rebel made a game of rumbling over the homeless men who bunked in the weedy grass, and tiny James Walker on Hudson Street, where we played ball in the snow at 4 AM after I'd finished driving my cab, cheered on by Norway rats the size of wildebeest.

Excitement was commonplace, even in Greenwich Village. On one occasion I foiled a car burglary, threatening to sic Reb, with his wagging tail and goofy demeanor, on the startled and not-so-bright thief. Another time, we chased a purse-snatcher down $8^{th}$ Street and held him at bay until the police came screeching to the rescue. And there was the day, on a Westside Pier, when I pried a terrified Poodle from the jaws of a snarling Malamute. I took six stitches for my efforts, while Eugenie and Reb watched from the sidelines.

We met our share of city dogs—a Setter named Shiloh and a pointer named Raff were Reb's favs-—but most of our pals walked on two legs, not four. Like the Lebanese brothers that owned the local deli. I don't remember how it started, but they took a liking to "Rappi" as they called him. They insisted that I bring him along whenever I stopped by. While I did my shopping, he'd sit by the counter as they chucked him remnants of ham, turkey, and other cold cuts that they had put aside just for him. If a customer dared complain about the unsanitary practice, he was told—not asked—to leave.

One gusty, autumn afternoon, Rebel and I were strolling down Commerce Street by the Cherry Lane Theatre. He had just finished scarfing down a mountain of bologna. I was babbling to him, cooing his nickname or some variation—Reb or Rebbie—as he did his business. While I stooped to pick up, I noticed a diminutive old woman headed my way. She was scowling.

"You should be ashamed," she said, wagging her finger and shaking her head. Her accent was European and thick, like Maria Ouspenskaya—"It is the pentagram, the sign of the wolf"—in the original *Wolf Man*. "Ashamed," she repeated, clearly waiting for an apology.

I shrugged, perplexed. I'd bagged the poop; what more did she want?

"To name the dog for the Rabbi and make fun!"

It took me a moment to process my transgression. Being a heathen, I'd forgotten that 'Reb' or 'Rebbe' means 'Rabbi' in Yiddish. I rushed to explain, but she waved me off and scuttled away, clucking in disgust.

Viewed through memory's gauze, New York seemed idyllic. It wasn't. Yes, Rebel, Eugenie, and I shared good times. But they were the exception, not the rule. I'd forgotten the ceaseless, mad scramble to survive, the long, dreary nights of thankless work punctuated by constant domestic strife.

When Rebel and Roxanne were lucky, most days they got three rushed trips around the block, often in stifling heat or freezing cold. The park was a special treat, the beach a rarity.

By comparison, Tanner was living the high life. So were we. Despite my nostalgic yearning, I would never go back. I didn't want to. This was exactly where I was meant to be, doing what I was meant to do, learning the lessons I needed to learn. Besides, even if I harbored a secret longing to relive the past, I no longer had the energy.

~~~

Along with Jack-o'-lanterns and too-early sunsets, fall brought the Santa Anas: powerful, dry "devil winds" that sweep down from the desert and pummel Southern California. Oftentimes they're merely annoying, overturning planters and aggravating allergies. Occasionally, they're deadly, igniting devastating wildfires. We've lived through several major blazes, one extinguished a few hundred yards of our home, and the roaring gusts always set us on edge.

Sometime after midnight, the winds kicked up and the trees started moaning. So did Tanner. He was seriously spooked, wide-eyed and shaking like he'd seen a ghost. He woke me every few minutes. I'd pry his quivering feet from my bed, tuck him back into his, and assure him that the big dog (me) would keep him safe. Then the wind chimes would clang or a door would slam and he'd freak out anew.

Hoping to stave off a total meltdown, I grabbed a blanket and curled up next to him on the floor. It didn't help. I crawled back into bed and invited him to join me. It didn't take much coaxing. Neither of us slept a lick. By morning, we were both bleary-eyed and out of sorts. Despite that, I found it reassuring, and ironic, that he'd turned to me for comfort and nurturing. Maybe I had a soft side after all.

***Refuge from the "Devil Winds***

The roaring winds left Tanner poised on the edge of a nervous collapse. My father-in-law shoved him over.

He and Sandra were in Malibu, shopping for orchids. Eugenie invited them for dinner. Tanner was resting when Gene barged in carrying a large carton. He was excited, shouting for his daughter to come see the wines that he'd selected. His boisterous entrance unsettled Tanner, who hid out in the bedroom until Gene calmed down.

We were just starting in on dessert when Gene swiped a cookie from his wife's plate and popped it into his mouth, mid-sentence. His lips kept moving but the words tailed off. He leapt up, tearing at his throat like a just-decapitated chicken.

"Relax! Swallow! Breathe!" Sandra was screaming at the top of her lungs.

Eugenie wrapped her dad in a bear hug and applied the Heimlich Maneuver. His face turned red, then ashen. His flailing grew more frantic.

I shoved Eugenie aside. I jammed my fist into Gene's chest and squeezed away. The guilty cookie flew out, but he continued to sputter and gasp like a drowning man. Finally, after several minutes, his breathing slowed. He collapsed back into his chair, drained.

Gene was out of danger but Tanner had lost it. He'd wedged his head under the coffee table, shivering like a skinny dipper at the North Pole.

If I'm tired or stressed—and thanks to Tanner and Gene I was both—I'll often take a turn on the "chi machine," a motorized device that gently rocks the user side to side, improving circulation and promoting relaxation. After my in-laws left, I plopped down on the floor, set the timer and shut my eyes.

As I lay wiggling back and forth, something cold and slimy brushed my ear. Tanner had slipped upstairs and was stretched out beside me, nuzzling my neck.

It tickled like hell, and I tried to shoo him away. He moved in closer and nestled up against me, the pair of us jiggling in sync. When the machine clicked off, we stayed together on the floor for a long while, just two dogs enjoying the moment and each other's company. It was heaven, and a sign that perhaps I'd finally turned the corner, that I was no longer too scary to live with.

~~~

Veterans Day was established by President Wilson to commemorate the truce that ended World War I. For Tanner and me it was also a day of redemption. Our first trip to Newport Beach had been an unqualified disaster. Tanner had heaved his guts out while his owner acted like a total psycho. But four months can make a world of difference for dogs. And men.

As we got ready to leave, Eugenie and I calmly reviewed our goal for the day: stay peaceful and try to have fun, no matter what. This time, I rode in back with Tanner. Whether it was my company or my new, improved attitude, he slept the entire way. There was no anxious panting, no frantic drooling and, praise Jesus, no barfing.

Like before, we met our friends at Fashion Island. Mindful of our July misadventures, we skipped the escalator in favor of the stairs. And we avoided the outdoor patio where we'd run afoul of the protocol police. We were hoping to show off Tanner's training, but, like a kid on a birthday party sugar rush, he was totally wired. He refused to heel, lunging after every dog we met, yet I stayed calm, gently correcting him like Tony had instructed.

By the time we left for home, my shoulder was on fire. My voice was trashed from chanting "No dog! No dog! No dog!" Nevertheless, when the garage door settled into place that night, I gave a silent cheer. We'd made it through a very challenging day without him losing his lunch, or me my composure.

Obedience training, the Santa Anas, the Newport do-over—I was on a roll. It felt like genuine progress this time, yet I pressed ahead, working to better understand my feelings and change my behavior. One tool was especially helpful in checking the harsh, critical judgments that ran through my mind, 24/7, like an all-bad news channel, stoking my anger. It was a simple mantra that I'd learned at Course In Miracles: "Just like me."

"Just like me" isn't really a mantra in the truest sense; it's an exercise in compassion and understanding. Instead of the harsh, limiting labels—stupid, greedy, fat, lazy, ignorant, rude, evil (fill in the blank with your favorite)—that we apply to people who don't share our judgments or act as we want, the mantra serves as a gentle reminder of our own flaws and the basic potential for goodness that's common to us all. No matter how lousy somebody's behavior might seem, and it can sometimes seem pretty awful, the people who bug us—a neglectful parent, a controlling spouse, an angry dog owner—are doing the best that they're capable of at any given moment. Even a judgmental hothead like me couldn't ask for more.

The real challenge lay in learning to extend that compassion and forgiveness to my harshest critic, myself. As far back as I could remember, every day had begun with scathing indictments from "The Voice," the inner judge that questioned and savaged my every action and intention. We all have one, but mine was particularly relentless, Inspector Javert on steroids. The moment I opened my eyes in the morning, it started in, insisting that whatever I had done or planned to do wasn't nearly good enough, and never would be. It dismissed my achievements out of hand and magnified even my tiniest failures. If I had written the Harry Potter series and earned a billion dollars like J.K. Rowling, "The Voice" would still have scoffed,

"Okay, you sold some books and made some dough, but you'll never be a real writer, not like Norman Mailer."

The relentless bombardment left me feeling drained, hopeless, and, well, angry. As I struggled to find a better, calmer way to be with Tanner, it dawned on me that I could do the same for myself. So one morning, when "The Voice" started to rip me, I simply told it to "Stop." If it had something to say, I'd listen later. First, I intended to walk my dog and have my coffee in peace. It took a week or so, but the son-of-a-bitch finally got the hint and backed off.

Sadly, anger wasn't my only negative form of expression. As a child, lashing out wasn't always possible or advisable. Instead, I learned to disengage from anyone who hurt my feelings, disappointed me, or otherwise pissed me off. When I couldn't retaliate, I'd tell myself that the offense, and the offender, didn't matter; that I could carry on just fine without them. Then I'd lock them away in an airtight compartment where they became invisible to me. Like Alec Guinness's Colonel in *Bridge on the River Kwai*, if I couldn't beat them with force, I'd best them with my iron will. I had plenty of practice with my father.

I lugged this coping mechanism into adulthood, and prided myself on my Zen-like detachment. Thanks to Tanner and some rigorous self-examination, I realized that my faux stoicism, like my anger, was just a misguided, unconscious attempt to suppress my fears. And it was totally unnecessary. Since I could choose how to see things, there was no one who could hurt me but myself. There was a happier, healthier way to live than going to war or shutting down.

My feelings toward animals, and dogs in particular, were far less complicated: I loved them passionately and always will.

*Enjoying State Street, Santa Barbara, with Tanner*

## NUMBER OF DOGS & PIT BULLS EUTHANIZED ANNUALLY

According to the Humane Society of the United States:
- ✓ There are approximately 3,500 animal shelters in the U.S.
- ✓ Of the estimated 6-8 million cats and dogs that enter shelters each year, approximately 2.7 million are euthanized and 3-4 million are adopted.
- ✓ Approximately 30% of all shelter dogs are reclaimed by their owners.
- ✓ Approximately 25% of shelter dogs are purebred.
- ✓ It is estimated that Pit Bulls make up approximately 40% of the dogs in L.A.'s 12 shelters and that 200 are killed each day in that city alone.

**Resources**

- The Humane Society of the United States
- Pit Bull Rescue Central

# CHAPTER 11
# THE HOLIDAYS

It's a rundown summer bungalow in a one-light town on Barnegat Bay. Compared to home, it's a palazzo on the Amalfi Coast. At least for us kids, who are free to fish, and crab, and swim, and roam the streets as we please, with no one to bitch that we make too much noise, or ruin the grass, or wreck the plants. For my mother, with no car and almost no money (she borrowed the rent from the corner grocer who has a crush on her), it's house arrest.

It's Tuesday, my father's day off. Instead of splashing in the bay, we're hanging around bugging her, asking when he'll be driving down from the city. She's anxious, not that there will be trouble—he's always calm whenever he visits—but that he'll fail to show and break our hearts again.

In the early evening, she crafts a fib about an "emergency" at dad's restaurant. We traipse to the local bar for shuffleboard and tomato pizza with oregano. We're long asleep when he swings by to drop off money for groceries and ice cream, an afterthought to his "date." They talk in strained, loveless whispers. When he's *gone, she sits on the jalousied porch, smoking Camels, fighting not to cry. She doesn't see me watching from the shadows, but I already know that people suck. Never let them see you care; too much pain that way.*

~~~

**Tanner and Taco**

Every Thanksgiving, before the feasting and football, Eugenie and I take time to consider just how fortunate we are. We have a beautiful home, good health, loving family and friends. And now we had Tanner. When we finished with our morning cuddles, we hopped out of bed and joined him on the floor where he lay basking in the sun. As we stroked his smooth, pink belly, we told him how grateful we are that he'd found his way into our lives.

Adopting the big, brown Pit had been a crapshoot. We'd taken a chance on a scary-looking throwaway dog and been richly rewarded. He'd brightened our world and drawn us closer together, something that we hadn't thought possible. In the process, my 4-legged teacher was giving me a lesson in fear and anger that was long overdue. Thanks to Tanner, I was learning to see the goodness in everyone, especially myself.

My father-in-law and his wife usually travel during the holidays, adding to their tally of 160+ countries. This year, for the first time in two decades, they were staying put, and they invited the entire clan, including Tanner, to their home for dinner.

We were cruising along Sunset Boulevard, not far from the house, when an accident forced us to detour onto the winding, neighborhood back roads. It was only a minor delay. That's all it took. As we were turning into Gene's driveway, Tanner retched and burped up his breakfast. I wasn't angry with him; he hadn't been carsick in months. If anything, I felt sorry that we'd ruined his winning streak. I soothed the dog and sent him off to play with Gene's cats while I mopped up. When I'd finished scrubbing down the car, we ran him through his commands for Eugenie's mom. Melissa was impressed, and she rewarded him with a cuddly, stuffed bear.

When my in-laws' friends, a sophisticated European couple, showed up with their toy Poodle in tow, things got interesting.

Tanner came racing to greet them. Oh, goody, a new friend! Clutching the fluffy dog to her chest, the woman recoiled in horror. That was perfect for Tanner, who was now free to sniff the little guy's patootie without getting nipped.

Eventually, the owners relaxed, and the pups got to socialize. After five minutes of fierce wagging and sniffing, they grew bored and retreated to the opposite ends of the table. They spent the rest of the evening ignoring each other, sucking up any crumbs that hit the deck. It was late when we left. Like many holiday revelers, Tanner slept all the way home, worn out from the day's excitement, and too much turkey.

~~~

On Black Friday, when most Americans go shopping, we argue about the Christmas tree. If I had my way, we'd put it up on Halloween and leave it there till Memorial Day. It's an irrational desire from childhood, when Yuletide meant a brief respite from the constant family turmoil. Eugenie is sympathetic, but she stalls me until early December and insists that it come down by Valentine's Day.

There's a special magic in the scent of a real tree. One whiff of a Scotch Pine or a majestic Douglas Fir and I'm seven again, scouring the Sears Catalog, scribbling Christmas lists, and baking cookies for Santa. Dogs aren't quite that nostalgic. For them, a real tree is just a handy porta-potty.

With that in mind, we skipped the walk down memory lane and settled for an unholy fiber optic "tree", a cross between a Chia Pet and a Lava Lamp. Tanner watched from his bed while we hung the ornaments and garland. We lugged a small mountain of gifts from the garage, dusted them off (thanks to Eugenie, they'd been wrapped since our Solvang trip), and deftly arranged them under the polyester bush, creating the perfect Hallmark moment. Then we left to have a glass of wine with some neighbors.

We came home to a scene from *The Terminator*. The tree was askew. The floor was littered with ornaments. Scraps of soggy wrapping paper were strewn about the room like confetti. In our brief absence, Tanner had clawed his way to the bottom of the pile where we'd stashed some plush dog toys.

From day one, he'd been gentle, even nurturing, with his "babies." Lately, however, he'd started savaging them at an alarming rate. The carnage began one evening when we went to a movie. He was fired up and wanted to play. We thought about bringing him along, but we weren't sure he could handle staying in the car alone. And there was always the puking thing. As we closed the door, he glared at us, annoyed at being left behind with so much fuel in his tank.

We returned to find his bed had been ransacked, the sheepskin throw torn to shreds. In the past, he'd accidentally ruined a few toys. With his shark-like jaws, some collateral damage was inevitable. This was clearly intentional. And he wasn't finished. In quick succession, he gutted Duckie, decapitated Blooie, and mangled his new bear, nicknamed *Un Occhio,* since he was now missing an eye. Sharpie somehow survived the rampage, but he was so disfigured that he could star in *Phantom of the Opera*.

Hoping to stem the onslaught, we bought Tanner a Konga, a thick, rubber toy the pet store clerk called "indestructible". He promptly trashed it…and four subsequent replacements. When I complained, the saleswoman threw up her hands.

"You might want to skip the toys," she said, "and just buy him an old Buick."

Like a delinquent who escalates from tagging to grand theft auto, Tanner moved from eviscerating stuffed animals to chewing Eugenie's favorite bedspread. Luckily, she caught him before he did much damage. She gave him a good scolding, his first, and, unfortunately, not his last.

The morning after his sneak attack on the linens, I was in the office checking e-mail when I heard him munching something in the bedroom. I poked my head in, and there he was, gnawing the same corner of the spread. Our mild-mannered dog was showing some 'tude, testing boundaries like a human teen. He quit the moment he saw me, but I went off, shouting "No, no, no!" and calling him a "Bad dog!" To make sure he got the message, I snatched him by the collar and shoved his face in the damaged fabric. He cringed and went flat, bracing himself for a beating.

That brought me up short. I would never hurt him, but how could he know that, especially given the abuse he'd already suffered? And why was he nibbling the spread in the first place? Maybe he was bored from lack of exercise. Or maybe it smelled like me. Or maybe the shiny satin caught his eye. It really didn't matter. This exquisitely sensitive dog needed firm but gentle correction, not intimidation. I let him down, turning a simple mistake into a contest of wills. Before I went back to the office, I folded back the bedspread so the sweet spot was out of reach.

It was Carl's birthday and I'd planned to surprise him with a special workout, a tai chi lesson. Instead of "waving hands like clouds," though, we sat in the breakfast nook, sipping tea and discussing human frailty. I told him about the chewing incident and my overreaction. He shrugged and suggested we use bitter apple to make the bedspread less appealing. Wise man.

~~~

We'd promised to spend Christmas with Eugenie's mom in Palm Springs. Two days before our visit, however, Tanner came down with a nasty case of pink eye. We don't have kids and weren't used to constant false alarms. We rushed to the vet who diagnosed it as seasonal, allergic conjunctivitis. She prescribed antibiotic eye drops and sent us home.

Tanner was a lamb in the office. When we tried to administer the drops, he went berserk, twisting and bucking like a rodeo bull. We backed off and phoned Dr. Lisa. She laughed and said to bring him in; her staff would do the heavy lifting. I rushed back to the office and handed him over to her assistant, a hefty young man who assured me it was "no big deal." He and Tanner disappeared into a back room. He returned a short while later, sweating and out of breath. I merely smiled and thanked him for his help.

On the morning of Christmas Eve, I took Tanner for an extra long hike to tire him out before the drive. He was bouncing like an AKC champion, glued to my side the way we'd practiced in class, when Dexter leaped out from the bushes. Caught off guard, Tanner reverted to his former exuberant, undisciplined self. I had to fight to get him under control. I was disappointed. So much for all that training. Dexter was grinning, pleased with the havoc that he'd wrought.

With Tanner's delicate stomach, stopping and starting was always risky, so we pushed straight on to the desert. We arrived at our hotel, vomit-free, around noon. We dropped our bags in the room, and then we trotted across the road to Melissa's new condo. Dudley met us at the door. We were stunned by how dramatically he'd aged since his last stay with us. He was gray all over now, blind in one eye, and hard of hearing. He walked with a limp and his breath smelled like week-old catfish. The old Pug still recognized us, though, and wagged his corkscrew tail in greeting. Spotting Tanner, he curled his lip and bared his stained, crooked teeth. He might be ancient but he was still the man of the house.

With Dud in the lead, we toured the grounds. There were the ubiquitous swimming pools, tennis courts, and citrus trees typical of desert communities...and a newly built dog run. When we let Tanner roam free at home, it was either at the beach or the park, where he could sidestep overly enthusiastic dogs. The fenced-in play area offered no escape from a neighbor's rambunctious Labs. Tanner is incredibly strong, but fending off two big, joyful brutes was more than he could handle. An hour of jumping, thumping, and humping and he was toast. We dragged him back to our room and left him there to recover while we joined some friends for margaritas. Everyone slept well that night.

Christmas day was cool and sunny, perfect for a long, leisurely lap around the complex and another episode of "Dogs Gone Wild." This time Tanner was rested and ready. He neutralized the rowdy Retrievers by backing into a narrow gap between a pair of trees, forcing them to abandon their tag-team assaults and face him single file.

Unlike the raucous *festas* of my youth, Christmas in the desert was a mellow affair, just the three of us, the dogs, Melissa's cat, and our friend M.C., who brought tinsel, garland and party favors—Santa hats for Eugenie and me and clip-on antlers for the pups. It would have made a terrific holiday picture, but we'd have had better luck ripping off the Russian Mob than getting Tanner to pose in costume.

Growing up Italian in New Jersey, Christmas dinner was a major production. My grandfather closed the restaurant and summoned the entire famiglia and several dozen friends for an all-day feast of mind-numbing proportion. It started with platters of antipasto, my grandmother's escarole soup, clams oreganata, and parmesan-stuffed artichokes. Then came baked lasagna, homemade ravioli, roast chicken, and grilled steak. For dessert, we had roasted chestnuts, fresh fruit, a mountain of torrone, cannoli, sfogliatelle, and struffoli, plus all the soda, beer, wine, and Asti Spumante that you could drink.

Attendance was mandatory. Boyfriends, in-laws, college pals—no excuse was accepted. Period. For this one day, the younger kids got to man the bar, serving up vile concoctions that no one in their right mind would taste, let alone consume. The teenaged cousins jitterbugged to "Jingle Bell Rock" on the jukebox, bemoaning the dates they'd been forced to break. My father and his brothers played cards and craps. The cheating was blatant and expected, accompanied by howls of feigned indignation. The seasonal bacchanals continued for a few years after my grandfather's death but, by then, the glue was gone and they eventually died out.

~~~

Take multiple vet visits, long car rides, a strange hotel room, and raucous play dates, mix them together and what do you get?

"I think Tanner pooped on the rug."

It was just past 3:00 AM when Eugenie shook me awake. The air reeked. I assumed it was just the fallout from a pungent doggie fart. I rolled over, but she insisted that I get up and check. I clicked on the light and saw Tanner scrunched down in his bed, looking guilty and ashamed. In the center of the white area rug was a steaming, runny pile.

Fighting hard not to barf, I hauled the ruined rug to the garage and dumped it in the trash. Then I tackled the carpeting, where the foul-smelling muck had seeped through. The blotting, soaking, and scrubbing took almost an hour. From the size of the detonation, Tanner had to be empty. Just to be safe, I took him outside. We stumbled around in the darkness until I'd cleared my nostrils. Then we returned to the scene of the crime. I papered the floor with doggie Depends, doused my covers with cologne, and crawled back into bed for a short, smelly night's rest.

The next day, Tanner seemed flat but otherwise okay. At bedtime, I urged that we cover the carpet with plastic drop cloths.

Eugenie pooh-poohed me. Tanner's bowels were back to normal, she insisted. Right. Sometime after midnight, he launched round two of "oops, it's poops." I wanted to scream "I told you so" and rub her nose in it. I wasn't really angry though; I was too busy gagging. Once again, I dug out the cleaning supplies and set to work. I was starting to feel like a hospital orderly.

The next week was rough on all of us, especially Tanner. At the smallest grunt or grimace, we rushed him outside. To spare his system (and the rugs), we swapped his food for rice. And we cut off all treats. He was understandably bummed and confused, wondering what he'd done to merit such abysmal treatment.

Tanner was still out of sorts on New Year's Eve when we dragged him to my in-laws' for a black-tie party. Things got off to a dicey start. They met us at the door in a full-blown panic. One of their cats was MIA, presumed to have escaped when Gene left the door ajar. Clad in gowns and dinner jackets, the four of us scoured the yard in vain. It was looking bleak—they live on heavily trafficked Sunset Boulevard—when Eugenie found the fugitive feline curled up in a closet.

The kitty was safe, but the frantic search had Tanner unnerved. It only got worse, with Sandra clanging about in the kitchen fixing dinner, me skulking around with my new camcorder, and the guests all wearing creepy party hats. The coup de grâce came when someone proposed a toast to "Auld Lang Syne." Gene uncorked the bubbly, Sandra fired off a party popper, and Tanner lit out for the second floor, where we found him cowering in the dark alongside the cats.

On the way home, we reminisced about the year gone by and the juicy change-up that Fate had thrown us. Only last December, I was stoked at the prospect of getting another majestic Setter and recapturing my youth. Now we were in love with a cowardly Pit Bull that was dragging me kicking and screaming into a long-delayed adulthood. On the radio, the Rolling Stones were singing, "You can't always get what you want, but if you try sometimes you just might find, you get what you need." We made it home by midnight, watched the ball drop on TV and, bellies bulging, hit the sheets.

**Tanner about to dispatch Gumby**

# CHAPTER 12
# WATER, WATER EVERYWHERE

*I'm rehearsing with a friend in my apartment on West 4th Street, running lines for a show so far off-Broadway that it might as well be Omaha, when the call comes in: my father is dead, his heart having exploded while screaming at a customer in the middle of the dinner rush.*

*I'm jolted, but not in the way most people would think. We've been strangers for too long now, too much alike in our selfish rage for that. The ground has shifted and it's finally over, all the hurt, disappointment and resentment. Except, it's not, because I ache for a chance to do it over, and better, a chance I'll never have. It will take years before I'm clear of it, able to see that, like me, like all of us, he did the best he could with what he had.*

~~

*New Year's Day on Westward Beach*

We kicked off the New Year with a run on the beach at dusk. The road was littered with seaweed that the tide had washed up the previous night. The ocean was roiling, riled up from a recent storm. As the fiery winter sun dipped below the horizon, it transformed the sky into a colossal Rothko, with giant azure, crimson, and orange bands. Tanner pranced beside us, happy to be outdoors with his people on such a majestic day.

We returned to the house and gave him a quick bath. Then we went inside for supper.

We were just starting on the salad when Eugenie glanced up and shrieked, "He's going on the rug!"

I spun around and caught Tanner squatting by the coffee table. We took turns scolding him. Then Eugenie rushed him outside to reinforce the correction while I sopped up a small lake.

I drenched the rug with odor remover and hung it out to dry. It was a hand-me-down from Eugenie's mom, which got me thinking. I called her to ask if, by chance, Dudley had ever peed on it. She was indignant; her dog would *never, ever* behave so crassly. Apparently a chilling bath and a large dish of water had upset Tanner's normally impeccable control.

Two days later, we came home from the market and caught him, leg cocked, flooding the same spot. We were floored, and alarmed. Tanner had never urinated in the house before. Now he was brazenly marking at will. Coupled with his toy rampage and the diarrhea disaster, it seemed our perfect dog was starting to backslide.

We called our trainer and explained the situation. When Tony heard the details, he cackled. He hastened to assured us that Tanner wasn't regressing or acting out. The rug had belonged to Melissa and, by extension, her Pug. Tanner was merely "claiming" it the only way he knew how.

Tony's advice was unequivocal: "Lose the carpet."

We did, and the marking stopped.

~~~

Californians like to see themselves as intrepid pioneers that brave the elements and blaze new frontiers. In fact, though, when the roads turn slick, they ditch work, bag social engagements, and crawl along like anxious snails, swerving to avoid the tiniest puddles and stomping the brakes like Gene Hackman in *The French Connection*.

After several years of severe drought, the winter rains brought welcome relief to the parched L.A. basin. Welcome, that is, unless you were a prissy Pit Bull with a lingering case of the runs. Tanner was miserable. He spent the better part of two weeks dodging raindrops, pouting in his bed and ripping his toys apart out of boredom. As his caretakers, we were also held prisoner by the inclement weather, forced to time our walks to avoid the heaviest downpours.

Compared to Setters with their long feathery coats, Pit Bulls are low maintenance, wash-and-wear dogs. They don't really shed, and their short, dense fur never needs trimming. Unfortunately, it doesn't offer much insulation either. So, when things turned damp and chilly, Eugenie insisted that we get Tanner a sweatshirt.

I was against it. Some people get a kick out of dressing up their pets, like my wife and her mother did with Dudley. To me, the animals look uncomfortable and, frankly, embarrassed. I noted that our weather is usually mild and that Tanner avoids the rain the way politicians avoid plain speaking, but Eugenie was adamant. To prove her point, she decked him out in one of her hoodies. Tanner looked cute as a cupcake, but the shirt distorted his gait, which is never a good thing if you're looking to avoid orthopedic problems. When he tried to navigate the stairs, he tripped and almost broke his neck. Before you could say "My dog's no sissy," he was back to his buff, naked self.

The sweatshirt was gone but Eugenie wasn't finished coddling Tanner. If the mercury dipped below 60 degrees, she broke out the space heater and swaddled him in a "snuzzy" (her word) designer blanket, a gift from profligate friends that cost more than our first bed. I found it ironic that she worried about him getting wet or cold. A year ago he was roaming the streets, sleeping who knows where and eating god knows what. Now he was Little Lord Fauntleroy.

While I laughed at her exaggerated devotion, it was effective. Lots of people practice massage, but few have the true healing touch like Eugenie, whose clients used to speak of her "gift" with saintly reverence. Although she no longer worked on humans, from day one she'd put her hand on the shaken dog and never stopped cuddling him. Tanner didn't like it at first; then he grew to tolerate it. Now, he craved her magic touch and blossomed because of it.

She'd done the same with me. Ignoring my angry outbursts and juvenile posturing, she focused on the kind, gentle spirit buried within. Whenever things went sideways, which was far too often, she'd stroke my chest, or cheek until the "fever" passed, telling me it didn't matter, that I was still special and her true love. In retrospect, she was right. Too bad it took me twenty-plus years to realize it.

~~~

In his gentle yet inexorable manner, Tanner had gotten me to change my sleep habits and confront my thorniest emotional issues. He was also forcing Eugenie and me to expand our geographical boundaries and to connect with our neighbors. For twenty years, we'd lived a quarter mile from the ocean and rarely gone to the beach. Except for some swing and salsa classes, we never visited the nearby Bluffs Park. Now in his brief tenure, we'd been there more times than all the previous years combined.

When friends drove down from San Francisco for a surprise visit, they brought along their Chocolate Lab. Teddy is bigger than Tanner and even more spirited. We wanted the dogs to play together, but where? The condo, with its fragile sculptures, was out of the question. Otto's owner, Bettina, suggested Escondido Beach, a pristine cove a quarter-mile away that we'd never bothered to explore.

We were nearing the entrance when we met a diver leaving with his catch, a six-foot-long "baby" shark that he'd hooked a few yards offshore. Watching Tanner and Teddy chase balls in the surf, I thought of *Jaws*, and the dog that disappeared retrieving a stick. I hoped baby's parents weren't lurking nearby, looking for some payback. Shark attacks are rare in Malibu but not unheard of. Shortly before we moved there, two kayakers disappeared into the belly of a Great White off Point Dume, a half-mile from our place.

When we first left New York, friends would tease that we'd gone soft, ditching the mean streets for peace and security. In all my time there I'd been robbed just once, while driving my cab, when two kids that I'd picked up outside an East Village club threatened to cap me if I didn't surrender the cash. They seemed like prep school posers, but I was tired and caught off guard. Instead of daring them to show me the chrome, I tossed them the wad of singles that I had stuffed in my pocket.

During our first year in California, we encountered coyotes, bobcats, and rattlesnakes. We even found a scorpion under our bed. Then, in quick succession, came the Rodney King Riots, the Northridge Earthquake, and the devastating Old Topanga Fire that ravaged Malibu, destroying 400 homes. Soon those same friends were pleading with us to quit the "jungle" and come home while we still could.

~~~

Eugenie and I are usually outgoing and pleasant; when I'm not pissed off that is. Nevertheless, we'd tried to keep our distance where neighbors were concerned. It was a throwback to our New York days, when we scrupulously avoided any social contact with the residents of our building.

Robert Frost said, "Good fences make good neighbors." That's especially true in Manhattan, where decent apartments, even tiny ones, cost a fortune and are brutally hard to find, and where it takes an act of God (or two) for people to even think of moving.

After a hectic day spent rubbing elbows with the huddled masses, that postage stamp, studio walk-up is your refuge. You're not about to muck it up by befriending the accountant/serial killer down the hall. Oh, she might seem sexy, charming and sophisticated at first. Let the chemistry turn sour, though, and you're stuck with a mortal enemy until one of you quits the premises or dies.

Despite our practiced reticence, we'd still managed to cultivate a few Malibu friendships. Suddenly, that slim roster was decimated by the financial crash of 2008 and subsequent mortgage meltdown. Our little corner of the complex was hit especially hard, with neighbors selling short, walking away, or being evicted. It was a sad, scary time, but Tanner helped us meet new people. We had no choice.

Dashing to collect the morning paper, you could slide by with a curt nod or a wave. Standing face-to-face while your dogs romped together, it was impossible to avoid trading homeowner scuttlebutt, sports talk, or political views with the people down the block. These casual conversations led to drinks, dinners, parties, and...new friends.

Through the dogs' schedules we came to know their owners' lives; who was sick, who'd changed jobs, or who was on vacation. I always worried when Tanner's doggie pals went AWOL, but he didn't seem to care; there was always someone else to play with. Then Trouble disappeared, and he was crushed. For weeks, he dragged me by their unit on every walk, trying to summon his Pit Bull sparring partner by sheer force of will. At first, I thought it just rotten timing or an extended holiday. Then one day I noticed a stranger padding about the empty condo. I was forced to break the news that his puppy BFF had moved away, another casualty of the housing crisis.

Tanner was still pining for Trouble when we learned that Sketch was gone, too. Her owner had surrendered her to a rescue group when he moved to a building that didn't allow pets. While dire circumstances can sometimes force people to abandon their animals, to voluntarily toss away a great dog like Sketch seemed unthinkable. We debated adopting her, but things were going so well with Tanner that we didn't want to risk it. It's difficult finding pet sitters for one dog. Who in their right mind would offer to watch two muscular Pits? And there was always the chance, however remote, that things could go south. Rebel was pure joy. Once we added Roxanne to the mix, life became way more stressful for him, and for us.

Around the time that Trouble and Sketch disappeared, our friends nearly lost Winnie. They took her shopping one afternoon and left her in the car with the windows open. It was a cool, sunny day, and they were gone only a short while. They returned to find her panting heavily, covered in spittle, a victim of heatstroke. They rushed to a nearby animal hospital where the vet administered life-saving emergency treatment. Had they been gone even a few minutes more, she wouldn't have survived.

~~~

Like us, Tanner had lost some buddies. Unlike us, he wasted no time making new ones. It seemed like everywhere we turned, we encountered new faces. There was "Coco", a sweet black Lab; "Priscilla", a dainty Cavalier King Charles; "Bruin", a hulking Bernese Mountain Dog; "Magoo", a slobbery English Bulldog pup; and "Jack" a tall, feisty hound. And that was just in our complex.

In nearly a year we'd never encountered a single stray. Now suddenly we crossed paths with a spate of runaways. First came "Buddha," a devilish Yellow Lab that we found running loose in Poop Park. I yoked him to Tanner, and we marched up the hill to his palatial home where the grateful maid thanked me for saving the dog and, presumably, her job.

Next there was "Mitzy." We were heading out for corned beef and green beer on St. Paddy's day when we spotted the zaftig Dachshund chugging toward us on the shoulder of the highway. We tried our best to coax her into the car. As dogs in danger are wont to do, she waddled out into the road instead. We peeled after her and managed to block four lanes of traffic without getting killed. I took up the chase on foot, and we finally cornered the elusive little snausage in a neighbor's garage.

Looking pleased as punch, Mitzy perched on my lap while we motored up and down the highway searching for the address on her collar. After several futile passes, we called the owner, who was out. We were prepping for a doggie sleepover when the UPS man drove by. Eugenie flagged him down. He recognized the address, which was next door to the churchyard, a mere quarter-mile away.

We leashed Tanner, and the three of us escorted the vagabond wiener back home. We found the doors unlocked, the windows open, the gate ajar. No wonder she'd escaped. We shut the house up tight, stuck Mitzy inside, and walked home. It was growing late, so we bagged our plans and settled for bottled Guinness and *The Quiet Man* on cable.

Finally, there was "Beau." We'd been to an Easter egg hunt at a friend's place in Beverly Hills. It was a crazy scene reminiscent of the Oklahoma land rush, with hordes of screaming kids frantically combing the grounds of the hilltop villa for a golden egg stuffed with silver dollars. We hung around for a while, enjoying the mayhem, then slipped out and hurried home to Tanner. As we were pulling into the complex, we passed a young black Lab walking distractedly on the sidewalk a few feet from the highway. His collar showed that Beau lived in a nearby unit.

While I was off searching for Beau's parents, Eugenie struck up a conversation with Dan, a writer-filmmaker who lives on the adjoining property with his wife, Kathryn, her son, Wynn, and their Weimaraner rescue, "Luna". We'd often seen them playing in the enclosed meadow that doubles as their yard.

"I wish Tanner could join them," Eugenie would say. A privacy-phobic ex-New Yorker, I never dared ask. Now that she'd been given an opening, though, Eugenie seized it. Dan said he'd be thrilled to have us, since Luna needed the socialization. We hurried home, slapped the leash on Tanner, and rushed right over.

It was love at first sight, at least for Tanner. He pulled out all the stops, sprinting, leaping, and wiggling his butt off, trying to entice the leggy hottie next door. Every time he approached, Luna barked and darted off as if he was the most loathsome creature on Earth. He pressed his case for almost an hour before we tossed in the towel and tore him away.

The next day, Tanner dragged me back to Dan's for another round of rejection. Luna hated him. She growled and bared her fangs whenever he came near. This went on for a week, with Dan and I trading movie reviews and Hollywood gossip while Luna rebuffed her relentless suitor. Finally, one morning, Tanner's persistence paid off. Luna stopped snarling, and she begrudgingly invited him to chase the slimy tennis ball that Dan was flinging. He was no match for the resilient game dog—her speed, stamina, and fielding skills would make a big leaguer weep—but Tanner was over the moon.

*Luna, the "girl" next door*

Despite the holiday hubbub, the bathroom mishaps, and the rotten weather, our timid, little prince kept making slow but certain progress. It still took forever to load him into the car, but at least he no longer barfed inside it. He was still wary of loud noises and quick movements, but he'd nearly stopped flinching. In a major coup that cost us a truckload of biscuits, Eugenie even taught him to roll over and lie still while we treated the scrapes and rashes from his rambunctious play.

As he grew more comfortable, Tanner kept adding to his bag of "cute dog" tricks. Every afternoon, as dinnertime approached, he would shift into what we call "countdown mode," acting extra playful and coy while nudging us in the direction of the kitchen, and his empty bowl.

To keep his shark-like choppers in good order, we gave him special tooth-cleaning bones for dessert, which we hid in the bedroom dresser. Whenever he heard the drawer squeak, he'd come tearing in and skid to a halt, sitting motionless, muscles tensed like a king cobra. To earn his prize, he would have to perform a simple command, like "come" or "sit." Out of the blue one day, Eugenie held the bone overhead and ordered him to "stand." Without a moment's hesitation, he popped up onto his haunches and balanced there until she forked it over. By the end of the week, he was slapping her palms when she asked for "ten". Tanner was eager to please and as smart as he was strong, the very traits that make Pit Bulls so charming, and so deadly in the wrong hands.

~~~

Day by day, Tanner was growing more relaxed and happier. The proof was in his tail. I was working in town and returned just as he and Eugenie were wrapping up their afternoon walk. When he saw me in the garage, he broke free and raced to greet me, his tail spinning round and round, whipping the air like a helicopter. He'd never shown that sort of unbridled affection before, especially not with me. We took it as a giddy sign that Tanner finally saw us as "his people," not just the saps that walked and fed him.

Seeing him every day, it was easy to forget how drastically he'd changed. Back when we first brought him home, a snapped twig or a scuffed shoe would've sent him flying. Now he could stay in "place" on a crowded soccer field, surrounded by dashing, screaming kids, and not freak out.

My evolution, while less dramatic, was still encouraging. The daily explosions hadn't altogether stopped—I could still be grumpy and reactive with Eugenie, especially before my morning coffee—but they were fewer now, and farther between. My habitual moodiness was slowly giving way to some new, unfamiliar feeling. Happiness? For the first time in ages, I was at peace, and we were all better off for it.

Tanner and I had come a long way, but we weren't totally out of the woods. Those old bugaboos, fear and anger, were still lurking about, just waiting for a chance to drag us backwards.

When Eugenie's mom downsized to a smaller condo, we inherited a truckload of her castoffs, including a new propane grill. As a "thank you," Eugenie offered to cook for Melissa the next time that she visited. Some guys treat grilling as a measure of their manhood. Not me. We never barbecued in New York and, thanks to my dad's restaurant madness, I don't enjoy cooking or culinary gadgets, particularly ones that require messy cleanup. When Melissa phoned to say that she was driving in from Palm Springs, I let Eugenie have at it while I went off to practice karate.

My wife's family has a special gene that renders them incapable of operating any and all mechanical devices. When she couldn't light the barbecue, I got the call. I rolled my eyes and hit the starter. It didn't fire. I tried again. It still wouldn't catch. After five minutes, the only thing heating up was my temper. Swearing under my breath in my filthiest Italian, I disassembled, cleaned, and reassembled the entire unit. Half an hour and a box of matches later, the grill finally sparked to life. I went back to my workout.

I'd barely broken a sweat when Eugenie popped in to say that the propane had run out. For a nano-second, I thought about heaving the sucker over the balcony. Tanner was watching, and so I calmly replaced the tank and re-lit the grill. By now, my rhythm was broken. Instead of forcing the issue and making myself nuts, I went with the flow. I bagged my training and got cleaned up. As I stepped from the shower, Melissa called to say that she'd be two hours late.

Like learning martial arts or healing a damaged dog, this personal transformation business was proving to be a gradual, challenging process. As a novice, you learn a few techniques and think you've got it licked. As your awareness expands, however, you realize that you've barely scratched the surface and that you'll never attain true mastery unless you fully commit to the program. That means taking advantage of every opportunity to test your mettle and grow, be it lunch with your mother-in-law, or a run-in with a horny Shepherd.

On a chilly day in early April, Tanner and I were playing at the ball field when his collar snagged the tote that we use to carry his toys. He took off like a shot, zigzagging in a frantic, futile attempt to escape the "demon" that flapped in the wind a foot behind him. I roared so hard that I cried. When I finally stopped laughing, I chased him down and unhooked the plastic banshee. The poor dog was terrified and couldn't stop shaking. I quickly packed up our gear, and we started back to the car.

We were almost to the parking lot when a large German Shepherd came charging toward us. His owner was nowhere in sight. I moved to intercept the dog, but he easily dodged me. He hopped on Tanner's back and started humping away. Tanner growled and tried to shake loose, but Shep held tight, grinding like a porn star.

I was struggling to separate them (without being violated or losing my fingers), when the owner finally sauntered over. I pointed to the sign insisting that dogs be leashed. He grinned and told me to "chill."

"Chill? Leash your freaking dog," I growled, "or I'll mount you and see how you like it!"

His smile faded. He tethered his dog and stalked off.

I put Tanner in the Prius and hurried after him. He saw me coming and wheeled around, bracing for a confrontation. I threw up my hands in surrender.

"I'm not looking for a fight," I said. I briefly recounted Tanner's history as a stray.

"I was just watching out for my dog," I explained. "But I overreacted, and I apologize." Then I turned and walked back to the car.

After a long, peaceful stretch, I'd lost my cool. I'd let my fear, of possible vet bills, lawsuits, and a black mark against my blameless Pit Bull, get the better of me. *That jerk thinks he's special...he doesn't follow the rules...his dog is out of control!* It would have been so easy to let "the story" escalate, and to use it to justify my anger. Instead of reverting back, though, I'd checked myself and quickly regained control. I wasn't Gandhi or Mother Teresa, but I knew then that the battle had turned.

That afternoon, when we opened the mail, we found a notice from the County asking us to renew Tanner's license. We were stunned. Had it been a year already? We dug out his records to check. The shelter photo showed a timid, malnourished dog trying to make the best of a dreadful situation. Along with the intake form and a brief medical history, there were handwritten notes from the staff: "Walks well on left side…Loves to play… Sweet disposition." Reading their comments, we realized once again just how lucky we were to have found this jewel of a dog before time ran out.

**Tanner's "snuzzy" sweater**

## *DOGS & HEATSTROKE*

Dogs regulate their temperature chiefly through panting. Heatstroke occurs on hot, humid days when they can no longer maintain a normal body temperature of approximately 101 degrees F. It can strike suddenly, and if your dog's temperature rises to 105 F or above, you must act immediately. If not, his internal organs will begin to breakdown and he may die. Even if you are able to lower his temperature, he may still suffer irreversible internal damage.

**Symptoms**
- A dog suffering from heat stroke will exhibit the following, progressive symptoms:
- Rapid panting
- Warm, dry skin
- Pale gums and a bright red tongue
- An anxious expression or disorientation (blank staring, an inability to respond to its name)
- Increased heart rate, thick, clinging saliva, vomiting, difficulty breathing.
- Collapse, coma, and death follow shortly thereafter.

**Treatment**
- Heat stroke often occurs when a dog is left outside on a hot day in direct sunshine or confined in a car, kennel, or crate. It's urgent to quickly reduce the dog's body temperature. To do this:
- Remove your dog from the car, kennel, or wherever he was confined and get him to a place with cool, circulating air, like an air-conditioned room.
- If possible, immerse him in a cool (not cold) bath, or hose him down. DO NOT leave wet towels on your dog and DO NOT use very cold water. Both can prevent your dog from cooling himself. Ice packs may cause hypothermia.
- To promote blood flow, gently massage the skin and flex the legs.
- While you're working to cool him, it's essential that he be transported to a veterinary hospital as quickly as possible. Even if you manage to reduce your dog's temperature, take him to the vet for a thorough exam, since serious internal damage to your dog's organs might have taken place.

**Prevention**
- ✓ On hot, humid days, or days with strong sun, NEVER leave your dog in an unattended car.
- ✓ Keep your dog indoors during the heat of the day in a well-ventilated or air-conditioned room. If your dog must be outside, make sure he has cold water, shelter, and shade.
- ✓ Since dogs really don't know their limits, try and keep your dog's activity to a minimum. If you must exercise your dog, do it in the early morning or evening when temperatures are generally cooler.

**Dogs Prone To Heatstroke**
- ✓ Young puppies, older dogs, overweight dogs, sick dogs or dogs recovering from illness or surgery.
- ✓ Short-faced breeds, like Bulldogs, Shar Peis, Boston Terriers, and Pugs.
- ✓ Cold climate dogs like Malamutes, Huskies, Great Pyrenees, and Newfoundlands.
- ✓ Double-coated breeds such as Pomeranians, Samoyeds, Collies, Shelties, Akitas, and Chow Chows.

## Resources

- Dr. Howie Baker, DVM
- American Veterinary Medical Association
- Christine Cadena, "Canine Protection: A Guide to Prevention and Treatment of Heat Exhaustion in Dogs"

**Tanner: American Staffordshire Terrier**

# CHAPTER 13
# FULL CIRCLE

The bath is running when I step away to answer an email from a friend urgently trying to find a home for another unwanted Pit Bull. I'm caught up in the search, thinking of Tanner, hoping this dog will fare as well, or at least not be put down. When I return, I freeze in horror. The bathroom floor is a lake; the bedroom carpet is waterlogged. Adrenalin surges, my head spins. I shut my eyes. Please be a dream, a terrible mirage, and not another stupid, careless mistake like the accident two days before, when I rear-ended another car that stopped short, while driving back from work with the sun in my eyes.

I rush to fetch Eugenie who is sanding marble in her studio. She's stunned, and upset. "Money's tight, and we're working so hard…" Am I trying to ruin us? She's not alone; the Voice is chirping, too: "Bum…Loser…Idiot…Moron." It's an explosive scenario, the kind that always sends me over the edge. Or used to.

I break out towels and mops, sopping up the moat that used to be our bedroom. I bail furiously but it's no use; the experts with *their vacuums and blowers will have to come and set things right for a sum that could buy clothes, lobster dinners, a weekend in Napa. Eugenie wrings her hands. Her face is pinched, despairing. I take her in my arms and stroke her golden-copper hair. It's my fault; she should be sore but it's not the end of the world. Not even close. Today's disaster will be next week's annoyance, a dinner party yarn a year from now. Besides, we have each other, and Tanner, who comes to join the party, tail swishing giddily, his new plush turtle clenched between his teeth.*

"You can't always get what you want… but sometimes you get what you need."

Writing about Tanner and the hurdles that we faced proved to be as difficult as I feared; it was one of the hardest labors that I'd ever undertaken. After months of floundering and cursing (I swore only when Tanner wasn't around, and then mostly in Italian), a book had finally started to emerge from my foot-high stack of musings. I badly wanted our story to have a big, dramatic Hollywood ending, but Tanner and Life weren't cooperating. So I considered staging a moving finale. It would have Tanner returning to the shelter for a homecoming visit on the day of his one-year anniversary, a shining symbol of hope and success. Of course, his loving, selfless owners would get their share of the credit, too.

As the big day approached, however, I began to have misgivings. They say that, unlike their human guardians, dogs live perpetually in the present, with no real sense of the past. I'm not so sure. Anyone who's ever had a dog knows that they certainly seem to remember people and places, especially ones that make a strong impression on them. The shelter was the start of Tanner's story. With a few bad breaks, it could just as easily have been the end.

Maybe someday we'll go back and let him share his triumph with the volunteers. We weren't ready for that just yet, and so I scrapped my plan. Instead, Eugenie packed a Tuscan supper, and we bundled Tanner into the car for a sunset picnic. As we were driving to the beach, we passed a couple in a white convertible riding with the top down. Perched behind them, on the rear seat, was an Irish setter. Head held high, snuffling the ocean air, the sight took me back twenty-five years to the beginning of our courtship, and Rebel, riding sandwiched between me and Eugenie on the ferry, as we crossed Long Island Sound to visit friends on Fire Island.

I also thought of Reggie. Could it be him, this healthy, well-behaved animal? The odds were crazy, but it pleased me to think that it was our wild child, out for a ride with his new vet owner and a beau, cured of his ailments and finally at peace. If we caught them, I planned to ask about the dog. Maybe he and Tanner would actually get to play. But the light stayed green, they drove on, and we turned into the parking lot.

Like people, dogs are subject to the whims of Fate. The same day that we plucked Reggie from the kennel in Upland, an anonymous woman pulled into the Agoura Hills Shelter and surrendered two Pit Bulls that she claimed to have found wandering on Pacific Coast Highway in Oxnard. One was a feisty, little gray female named Nadia that had just given birth, the other, a timid, underweight, brown and white male named Tanner.

~~~

Despite some anxious moments (and oceans of drool and vomit), our first year with Tanner went by like a sneeze. Watching him bounce along on our walks, it's hard to recall the skittish rescue dog that used to slink behind me, head hung low, bracing for the danger that loomed at every turn, the malnourished stray that ate in fits and starts, stopping constantly to check for unseen assailants.

Now he gobbles down his food without a glance. Then he runs to fetch his toys, kicking off each day with affection and exercise instead of threats and abuse. He has grown buff from all that exercise, packing on ten pounds of rippling muscle. He prances proudly, eager to demonstrate his tricks for anyone willing to fork over a treat, or two. Sorry, Tony. He used to pull and strain to greet other dogs. Now he sits patiently (okay, not all that patiently, especially with puppies), until we signal that it's okay to play, which he does with a gusto and good nature that never cease to amaze me.

The homeless dog that slept on the street or, when he was lucky, on a tattered shelter pad, now bunks down in one of three comfy beds, nestled in plush blankets. He's still obedient and respectful of our boundaries, but he's welcome on the sofa any time and, when the Santa Anas rage, on my side of the bed as well.

It seemed to take forever, but Tanner eventually made peace with the car. He rides up front with us now, or at least half of him does, his butt resting on the rear seat and his torso on the console so that he can crawl into my lap if things get shaky. He still has issues with the wind and the rain, but we're working on those, too.

Some of his doggie pals have moved on (Trouble and Sketch), and some have passed on (Shiloh, Winnie, Dudley & Ceba), but Tanner continues to make new friends, human and canine, everywhere he goes. If he's not tussling with Dexter, cruising the meadow with Luna, or tearing up the beach with Charlie, he's snoring away at Course In Miracles, the unofficial ambassador of non-human consciousness.

Or you might find him at the new Malibu dog park, leading a gang of the 4:00 PM regulars in a manic game of "catch-me-if-you-can," spreading the gospel that Pits can make great pets, and trusted, loving companions. We were there for the grand opening, which followed a decade of planning and legal wrangling. An acre-sized playground with an obstacle course, shaded gazebo, and security gates to rival a federal lock-up, it was packed with scores of dogs from Danes to Chihuahuas. Tanner adored them all and they adored him back, with one exception—an ornery little Dalmatian-mix appropriately named Lou.

Maybe one day, I'll undertake a sequel, detailing Tanner's transformation from adored family pet to healing therapy dog, agility champ, and canine savior of mankind. For now he's happy and thriving, and that's more than enough.

~~~

If we "saved" Tanner, he returned the favor, at least for me. I still sputter more than I should but not nearly as often, or as forcefully, as before he came to live with us. The volcanic outbursts and nightmares that plagued me since childhood are largely a thing of the past. On the rare occasion that I suffer a relapse, I look at Tanner and Eugenie and catch myself before things get too gnarly.

Living with Tanner has helped me to reconnect with my softer, more playful self. Thanks to him, I've learned how good it feels to suspend my judgments and self-criticism and, like a dog, just "be." I've come a long way but, to quote Robert Frost, "I have miles to go before I sleep." Like Tanner, I'm a work in progress. Aren't we all?

# **THE END**

# ACKNOWLEDGEMENTS

Many people helped make this book and my transformation possible:

- The Agoura Hills (L.A. County) Animal Shelter for keeping Tanner safe until he joined our family.

- Kathryn Galán for her editing expertise and formatting prowess without which this book wouldn't exist.

- Dan Cohen, Davidson Garrett, Joe and Linda Simone, dear friends, talented writers, and sharp-eyed readers for their whose encouragement and immensely helpful suggestions.

- Gary Horn, my pal, screenwriting partner and fellow curmudgeon for insisting I keep on scribbling no matter what.

- The late Caren Bohrman, a terrific agent who loved her writers, even the temperamental one.

- Dr. Judy Dunn, Dr. Zari Hedayat, Dr. Andrea Brandt, and Dr. Fran Walfish for their invaluable insights into human psychology.

- Pepperdine University Professor Dr. Ginger Rosenkrans and her Advertising 475 students for their help with cover and website design (Jesse Segura, Timothy Mitchell, Madii Laferney, Megan Duncan, Adam Goff), book trailers and PSA ( Klara Tomkins, Katrina Kirsch, Isabella Gonzalez, Rylee Baisden, Jing Huang) and with tradition and digital advertising strategies (Tori Vollmer, Ross Seeman, Justin Cumbee, Caitlin Doud, Christy Panchal, Kathleen Skoczylas, Lauren Rice, Cathy Lee, Vicky Liu).

- Danny Duchovny for giving Tanner a human voice.

- Our friend Avesta Cararra of the Pepperdine Alumni Affairs Office for introducing us to Ginger and her class.

- The late Tony Rollins, Tanner's trainer, for helping him and me reach our full potential.

- Dr. Lisa, Dr. Dean, and the staff at Malibu Coast Animal Hospital for keeping Tanner healthy and happy.

- Rob Lerner, CPDT-KSA, and Howie Baker, DVM, for their help with the sidebars.

- Sensei Andy Diaz and Sensei Mel Pralgo whose instruction and wisdom kept me from going over the edge.

- My in-laws Melissa, Gene & Sandra, Stephanie & Ernie and their son, Armand, for their love and encouragement.

- My parents for the lessons they helped me learn.

- My sisters, Honey and Mary, and my brother, Tony, who rode the childhood rapids with me, for their emphatic love and support.

- Debrah Caraway for her rescue efforts and the photo collage of Tanner.

- Carl, Roberta & 'Charlie', Robby, John & 'Lola' and 'Porter,' Zari, Ahmad & 'Dexter', Dani, Rich & 'Kona', Doug, Jean & 'Ceba', Bettina & 'Otto', and the crew at Malibu Dog Park for graciously sharing their friendships and toys with us.

- Ed King and the gang at A Course In Miracles for taking me into the fold and helping me "see things differently."

- Tanner, an amazing dog, terrific companion, and my 4-legged therapist, for his gentle, healing, soulful nature that helped me discover my better self.

- Finally, Eugenie, my wife, best friend, and the love of my life, for always believing in me when I didn't deserve it and sticking by me until I saw the light.

# APPENDIX #1
# DOG RESCUE RESOURCES

There are thousands of private and public rescue organizations, some of which are devoted to specific breeds, like Irish Setter Rescue. Pit Bull Central offers a nationwide listing of shelters that have Pit Bulls available for adoption. In addition, many cities and states have humane associations. The following is a partial list of resources:

- American Humane Association
- Animal Rescue League of Boston
- Animal Rescue New Orleans
- Bad Rap
- Best Friends Animal Society
- C.A.R.L. (Canine Adoption & Rescue League)
- Dogs Deserve Better (DDB)
- Downtown Dog Rescue
- Elayne Boosler's Tails of Joy
- Greyhound Pets of America
- Helen Woodward Animal Center
- Home for Life
- Houston SPCA

- Humane Society of the United States
- Karma Rescue
- Last Chance for Animals
- Liberty Humane Society
- Linda Blair WorldHeart Foundation
- Los Angeles Animal Services (LAAS)
- Maddie's Fund
- Marin Humane Society
- MuttShack Animal Rescue Foundation
- Nashville Humane Association
- New Leash on Life
- No Animal Left Behind
- Noah's Wish
- North Shore Animal League (NSAL)
- Out Of The Pits
- PAWS-LA
- People for the Ethical Treatment of Animals (PETA),
- Petfinder
- Pet Savers Foundation
- Saint Martin's Animal Foundation
- Southern Animal Foundation
- SPAY/USA, 1-800-248 SPAY (7729)
- St. Francis Animal Sanctuary

# APPENDIX #2
# ANGER MANAGEMENT RESOURCES

It worked for me, but not everyone should use a Pit Bull as a therapist. For people interested in more traditional approaches to anger management and peaceful living, here's a brief list of organizations, books and people that might offer some guidance.

- The American Psychological Association
- The Southern California Counseling Center, 323.937-1344
- National Anger Management Association
- American Association of Anger Management Providers
- *Living Beyond Anger: Living With Love* by Andrea Brandt, PhD, M.F.T., Santa Monica, CA, 310.828-2021
- *Calming The Family Storm: Anger Management for Moms, Dads and All The Kids* by Gary D. McKay, Ph.D. & Steven A. Maybell, Ph.D.
- *Stop The Anger Now: A Workbook for the Prevention, Containment, and Resolution of Anger* by Ronald T. Potter-Efron

- *The Anger Management Sourcebook* by Glenn R. Schiraldi, Ph.D. & Melissa Hallmark Kerr, Ph.D.
- *The Anger Solution* by John Lee
- *A Course In Miracles*, published by the Foundation for Inner Peace
- *Feel The Fear And Do It Anyway* by Susan Jeffers, Ph.D.
- *Taking the Leap: Freeing Ourselves from Old Habits and Fears* by Pema Chodron
- *When Things Fall Apart: Heart Advice for Difficult Times* by Pema Chodron
- *The Places That Scare You: A Guide to Fearlessness in Difficult Times* by Pema Chodron
- *The Anatomy of Peace* by the Arbinger Institute

LOUIS SPIRITO

# ABOUT THE AUTHOR

A lifelong dog lover and recovering "angry guy," Louis Spirito lives in Malibu, California with his wife, Eugenie, and their rescue Pit Bull, Tanner. A screenwriter, journalist, and playwright, his work has been honored by WorldFest Houston, The Nuyorican Poets Café, the Nicholl Fellowship Competition, Writer's Digest, and the Dog Writers of America. *Gimme Shelter* is his first non-fiction book and was awarded the indieBRAG Medallion.

Mr. Spirito is proud to donate 10% of all profits from this book to animal rescue groups that nurture and find forever homes for their beloved four-legged clients.

If you enjoyed GIMME SHELTER, you can follow Lou and Tanner's progress at:

**louisspirito.com**
**tannerthepitbull.blogspot.com**

www.ingramcontent.com/pod-product-compliance
Lightning Source LLC
LaVergne TN
LVHW051549070426
835507LV00021B/2490